Mahatma Gandhi

Published with permission of Hulton Deutsch Collection Limited, Unique House, 21–31 Woodfield Road, London, W92BA.

Mahatma Gandhi

A Selected Bibliography

April Carter

BIBLIOGRAPHIES OF
WORLD LEADERS, NUMBER 2
GREGORY PALMER, SERIES EDITOR

GREENWOOD PRESS
Westport, Connecticut • London

Library of Congress Cataloging-in-Publication Data

Carter, April.
    Mahatma Gandhi : a selected bibliography / April Carter.
        p.   cm.—(Bibliographies of world leaders, ISSN 1056–5523 ;
    no. 2)
    Includes indexes.
    ISBN 0–313–28296–X (alk. paper)
    1. Gandhi, Mahatma, 1867–1948—Bibliography.   I. Title.
II. Series.
Z8322.7.C37   1995
016.95403′5′092—dc20   94–46929

British Library Cataloguing in Publication Data is available.

Library of Congress Catalog Card Number: 94–46929
ISBN: 0–313–28296–X
ISSN: 1056–5523

First published in 1995

Greenwood Press, 88 Post Road West, Westport, CT 06881
An imprint of Greenwood Publishing Group, Inc.

Printed in the United States of America

The paper used in this book complies with the
Permanent Paper Standard issued by the National
Information Standards Organization (Z39.48–1984).

10 9 8 7 6 5 4 3 2 1

Contents

Introduction

This bibliography covers Gandhi's life, his political campaigns and his philosophy of nonviolence and strategy of nonviolent action. It also includes assessments of his historical significance and references to the Gandhian movement since 1948. It is a selective bibliography, which includes the major works on Gandhi's life and thought and aims to present critical as well as sympathetic or admiring accounts. It does, however, list books and articles that appeared throughout Gandhi's life, some of which are slight in content, in order to show how Gandhi was presented to the West at various stages of his career and the kind of impact he had. It also includes quite a number of books based on memories of those working with Gandhi or meeting with him.

Gandhi's life and actions from 1915 were inextricably linked to the evolving movement for Indian independence, and in order to understand Gandhi it is important to understand his relations with other major figures in India up to 1948. There is therefore a section covering biographies of Gandhi's contemporaries, and references are given to Indian National Congress materials, though these are not of course exhaustive. Second, in order to assess Gandhi's personal impact and the effectiveness of his campaigns it is also necessary to see how those in government in both South Africa and India responded to him, so relevant diaries, memoirs, biographies and government reports and archives are indicated. Since some researchers may be primarily interested in Gandhi's impact on British government policy-making on South Africa or India, some relevant materials on British prime ministers and other key officials are listed. So are the primary sources available.

A third consideration in compiling this bibliography has been Gandhi's importance for unofficial groups in the West, for example, campaigns to end colonialism, peace organizations and those interested in radical social or spiritual change. Therefore books have been included that indicate Gandhi's links with such groups and his influence upon them. The analyses of Gandhian thought also extend to interpretations of nonviolence by Western theorists and activists which do not always adhere closely to Gandhi's own interpretation.

Since this bibliography is directed primarily toward English-speaking readers in the West, it omits many of the writings on Gandhi published in India in both English and Indian languages. Several much more exhaustive bibliographies on Gandhi have been produced earlier by Indian scholars (see Section XII). Since, however, many of the key works on Gandhi have naturally been written by Gandhi's colleagues, or by Indian historians or political scientists, and these works are available in many university libraries in the English-speaking world, a significant number of books published in India have been incorporated.

Virtually all the books included have been annotated to indicate the nature of the content or the significance of the author. In a few cases the title is self-explanatory or the author's significance has been explained elsewhere. There is some cross-referencing to other items in the bibliography. Articles have not been annotated unless there is a special reason for commenting upon them.

A few articles in French or German have been referenced, but this is almost wholly a bibliography of books and articles in English, or translated into English.

Mahatma Gandhi

Summary Biography of Mahatma Gandhi

Introduction

Mohandas Karamchand Gandhi is widely recognized as one of the major political figures of the twentieth century, and as the father of independent India, although he never held government office. He was revered by many in India as a saint and was an inspiration to many others in the West. His uniqueness lay in his ability to combine his moral appeal with shrewd political leadership.

Gandhi first became widely known through his campaigns in South Africa in the years before the First World War, when he led the Indian community in nonviolent resistance to discriminatory laws. When he returned to India in 1915 he was 45 years old, and during his 21 years in South Africa he had become an accomplished political organizer, propagandist and tactician. He had developed his distinctive theory and practice of nonviolent action (satyagraha) and his own social theory, which rejected many aspects of Western civilization. As he relates in his *Autobiography*, Gandhi had during his South African years pursued his lifelong interest in religion and his quest for the right way to live; and so he evolved the ascetic, community-based lifestyle which distinguished his leadership in India. His spiritual qualities were recognised by the Indian poet,

Rabindranath Tagore, who bestowed on Gandhi the title of "Mahatma" or "great soul."

Gandhi gained a wide political following in India during 1917–1918 through a national campaign against indentured labour and campaigns against local injustices, and between 1919 and 1922 became the leader of the national independence movement. He remained a key figure in the struggle for independence and in negotiations with the British until the creation of independent India and Pakistan in August 1947, although in the last year of his life his main concern was trying to stop the communal riots between Hindus and Muslims, which were leading to appalling bloodshed. His death in January 1948, when he was shot by a Hindu extremist, heightened his image as martyr and saint.

By the 1920s he had a devoted band of admirers, both Indian and European, and the early biographies began to spread the idealised legend of the Mahatma. After his death the Government of India sponsored the publication of Gandhi's *Collected Works*, and his followers issued numerous editions of his writings and accounts of his life and campaigns. Scholars have therefore had to look behind the cult of Gandhi for the real man, though contemporary journalists and personal associates have provided vivid impressions of his personality.

Gandhi's life was full of apparent contradictions. The political activist often credited with destroying the British Raj was, for the first 50 years of his life, a loyal subject of the British Imperial Crown. The apostle of nonviolence acted during the First World War as a recruiting officer for the British army. The man who, in later years, wore only a loincloth and a shawl, and worked untiringly for the poor and the outcast, was the close friend of millionaires. The Hindu who drew heavily on his culture for inspiration was, at the same time, critical of many aspects of Hinduism (especially the caste system) and remarkably cosmopolitan and eclectic in his approach to religion and in his social beliefs. The lifelong advocate of religious tolerance, who strove to reconcile

Hindus and Muslims, eventually—though very reluctantly—endorsed the creation of the separate Muslim state of Pakistan.

Gandhi attracted controversy throughout most of his life, and has evoked very divergent assessments from historians and biographers since 1948. One contentious issue is whether Gandhi's strategy, which combined periods of mass non-cooperation and civil disobedience with negotiation and compromise, promoted or hindered the cause of Indian independence. Gandhi was opposed at various times both by Indian moderates, who wished to make progress through the constitutional reforms offered by the British, and by radicals, who believed that Gandhi's scruples about violence were holding back the momentum of the movement. Interpretations of Gandhi have also been influenced by historiographic debates about the role of the Indian nationalist movement. The Cambridge school of British historians has argued that Indian independence was being ceded rapidly because of the inner weaknesses of the British administration, and has interpreted the nationalist movement as a struggle for power within the Indian elite, not as a genuinely nationalist movement against British imperialism.[1] A recent strand in Indian historical writing, "subaltern studies," concentrates on the autonomous militancy of the peasants and workers, and so also regards all intellectual and political leaders of the nationalist movement as engaged in a self-serving power struggle.[2]

Gandhi's adherence to nonviolence has also attracted critical and often dismissive comment, especially in relation to his views on the possibilities open to the Jews facing Nazism and his advocacy during the Second World War of nonviolent resistance to the Japanese should they invade India. Marxists and socialists have attacked Gandhi for failing to support the political and economic measures, such as state control of the economy and expropriation of wealthy landowners and capitalists, they saw as necessary to tackle poverty. Many commentators have deplored Gandhi's rejection of most aspects of Western civilization, which they have seen as backward looking and obscurantist, tending to perpetuate the ills of Indian society.[3]

Attitudes in the 1990s are more sympathetic to Gandhi's ideas and lifestyle than they were 50 years previously. Popular movements of nonviolent resistance in many countries have shown how non-cooperation and civil disobedience can, in some circumstances, undermine repressive regimes. There is also much greater willingness to believe that non-Western cultures may embody values and understanding of the social and natural world from which the West could benefit. The green movement has challenged assumptions about the desirability of Western-style industrialization and continuous technological progress, and the disintegration of Soviet state socialism has required new thinking about how to achieve a just and democratic society. The literature on Gandhian thought, and on the philosophy and methods of nonviolent action, is therefore still growing.

Gandhi's Family and His Early Years

Gandhi was born in October 1869, the youngest son of Karamchand Gandhi and his fourth wife, Putlibai. The Gandhis came from the Modh Bania subcaste of the Vaisyas, who were originally small traders, probably grocers. But his grandfather, father and uncle were all prime ministers in various small princely states in the Kathiawad peninsula in northwest India—his father was prime minister first in Porbandar and later in Rajkot and Vankaner. The princely states retained some autonomy under the British Raj, although a British Resident was based at Rajkot to supervise the Kathiawad area, and Gandhi's father was very briefly imprisoned after protesting to an Assistant Political Agent who insulted the ruler of Rajkot. Karamchand Gandhi was an able official despite having virtually no formal education; he was also incorruptible and left very little wealth behind him when he died in 1886. Gandhi remembered his mother as deeply religious, visiting the temple daily and scrupulously keeping religious fasts.

The first major event of Gandhi's life was his marriage at the age of thirteen to Kasturbai. Gandhi regrets in his *Autobiography* his immersion in the sexual delights of the marriage bed at so early an age and his jealous and autocratic behaviour toward a rebellious Kasturbai. He also regretted that he never found the time to teach her to read and write.[4] Later he rejected the Hindu view of a wife as a "bondslave" and upheld the principle that she should be a free and equal partner "in all his joys and sorrows."[5] As a result of his own experiences Gandhi strongly opposed child marriages.

Gandhi was the only boy in his family to finish his high school education, so the family agreed to send him to England to study at the bar in the hope that he would in turn be qualified for holding high political office. When he sailed for England in 1888, the eighteen year-old Gandhi was paralysingly shy and not yet fluent in English. Because he had vowed to his mother not to eat meat, he almost starved on the boat journey.

In London Gandhi, who had defied the elders of his Bania caste when they tried to stop him from going abroad, showed his inherent tenacity. He eventually overcame the problems posed by his vegetarianism and achieved a tolerable diet. He walked many miles every day across London to save money on fares, and though not academically outstanding he studied hard and in 1891 passed the bar examinations. Gandhi had a brief fling at trying to become an English gentleman, took lessons in music and dancing and, according to an Indian student contemporary, dressed like a "masher" in high wing collar, a multicoloured tie and striped silk shirt. His fundamental seriousness drew him, however, to a discussion circle of Muslim students, to read religious texts, including the Bible and the Bhagavad Gita, and to study vegetarianism. This dietary commitment became an asset when it inspired him to start exercising his writing and organizing abilities—producing his first articles and founding a vegetarian club. Through vegetarianism he also met a congenial circle of liberal-minded British intellectuals, including

the well-known theosophist Annie Besant, later prominent in the
campaign for Indian independence.

When Gandhi returned to India in 1891 he did not, despite his
legal qualifications, have much success. He was still extremely
shy—he found himself unable to plead a case before the court when
he eventually got his first brief in Bombay—and he had still to learn
Indian law. He did begin to make a modest living in Rajkot drafting
legal petitions, but antagonised the British Political Agent by trying
to intervene on behalf of his brother over a political appointment.
The agent threw Gandhi out of his office and brought home to him
the power of the British in India. An offer by a Muslim firm of a
one-year job in South Africa to conduct a civil suit gave Gandhi a
welcome chance to escape from the intrigues and humiliations of
life in Rajkot. He sailed for Durban in 1893. Gandhi was parting
for the second time from his wife, Kasturbai, and leaving behind
his two sons, Harilal born in 1888 and Manilal born in 1892. The
young Gandhi seems to have been more reliant on his adored
mother—he had been deeply upset to return from England to
discover that her death had been kept from him. Biographers have
explored Gandhi's attitudes to his mother to account for the strong
feminine streak in his nature, indicated by his aptitude as a nurse
and his ideal of devoted self-sacrifice. Gandhi had greatly respected
his father, who died in 1886, but there was a fifty year gap between
them.

Critics of Gandhi have attacked him for his later treatment of his
wife and sons. The mature Gandhi made great demands on his wife,
who was required like other members of his experimental communities to do menial tasks she found demeaning. He did not consult
her about his intention to avoid further children by abstinence from
sexual intercourse until in 1906 he made a formal vow of chastity;
he says in his *Autobiography* that she "had no objection."[6] Moreover, the uneducated Kasturbai could not offer Gandhi the intellectual companionship and political support he found with some of his
women friends, in particular Madeleine Slade (Mira Behn), who

devoted her life to him and his causes after 1925. Nevertheless, Kasturbai loyally took part in satyagraha, presided over his ashrams, and followed her husband to jail in 1942. She died there in February 1944, and Gandhi sought an outlet for his grief in a flurry of letters to the British authorities about the treatment of his wife. He held a service to mark the day of her death each year until he too died. Gandhi's four sons were subjected to his unorthodox views on health and education, and he notes in his *Autobiography* that his sons had complained about the lack of formal schooling.[7] When adult they had to accept his patriarchal exercise of authority over when and whom they could marry. The three younger sons did adopt their father's ideals. Manilal, for example, took a leading role in the 1931 campaign against the salt tax, and later returned to South Africa to edit *Indian Opinion*. But the eldest, Harilal, rebelled and broke with his father in 1911, and later led an increasingly dissolute life.

Gandhi in South Africa

Gandhi's awakening to the systematic discrimination suffered by Indians in South Africa is described in every biography and was dramatised in Richard Attenborough's widely shown 1982 film *Gandhi*. When taking a train to Pretoria, in the Transvaal, Gandhi was roughly evicted from the first class carriage in which he was travelling. He protested to the railway company, and he also began to urge the Indian merchants and professional men in Pretoria to overcome their sectarian religious differences and to prove themselves deserving of equal treatment with whites.

When Gandhi arrived in South Africa in 1893 it was divided into the British colonies of the Cape and Natal Province, and the independent Boer republics of Transvaal and the Orange Free State. Growing British imperial ambitions in the 1890s and increasing Afrikaans nationalism led to the Boer War in 1899. Gandhi at this stage saw himself as a loyal subject of the British Empire and he also believed, when he came to engage in political action on behalf of the Indians, in the possibility of appealing to the liberal principles of the British. There was a substantial Indian population of indentured labourers on fixed-term contracts, brought into Natal to work on the sugar plantations and later in the mines. They often chose to stay on, despite being required to pay a poll tax and other forms of discrimination. There were also increasing numbers of "free" Indians, who travelled to South Africa primarily to make a living as traders, who were seen as a threat by the whites in the cities. In the 1890s the largest number of Indians (about 50,000) lived in Natal, almost the same number as whites in the province. There were around 10,000 Indians in the Cape and about 5,000 in Transvaal. The Orange Free State had expelled Indian traders and almost totally excluded Indians. The treatment of Indians in the Boer republics of Transvaal and the Orange Free State was extremely discriminatory: Indians could only take up menial jobs such as being waiters, and they were confined to certain areas and subject to a curfew.

Gandhi used his first year in Pretoria to document the conditions of Asians in the Transvaal, to encourage the middle-class Indians in Pretoria to assert their rights, and to study the case he was employed upon in depth. He was able to persuade both parties to settle out of court and save heavy legal expenses. He then returned to Durban and was about to sail for India, when he discovered that the Natal Government planned to introduce a bill to disenfranchise Indians. The Durban Indian merchants persuaded Gandhi to stay and fight their cause; as an Indian barrister with a good knowledge of English he was well placed to do so. Gandhi organized a petition against the bill. When the Natal Legislature passed it, Gandhi then made use of the fact that the bill still required the Queen's assent to organize a much bigger petition of 10,000 signatures (virtually all the Indians in Natal) and to send numerous copies to officials and newspapers in both Britain and India.

Gandhi decided to remain in Natal to combat the legal and social discrimination against the Indians, founded the Natal Indian Congress and started to practice law on behalf of the Indian community. In 1896 he returned to India to bring back his family and to promote the cause of the South African Indians in India itself. He wrote a pamphlet on the issue which was well publicised and sold widely and also addressed large public meetings sponsored by prominent Indian politicians, who were willing to unite on this cause despite ideological differences. Distorted news reports about Gandhi's activities in India aroused hatred in Natal; when he returned to Durban in January 1897 he was attacked by a mob of Europeans, and was fortunate to be rescued by the wife of the police commissioner, who happened to be passing.

When the Boer War broke out, Gandhi decided that the Indians of Natal should demonstrate their loyalty as citizens of the British Empire, despite their lack of citizen rights. He managed to persuade his compatriots to accept this point of view, but the British were reluctant to make use of the services of untrained Indian volunteers. Eventually, however, as British casualties grew, the government agreed that an Indian Ambulance Corps should be created; 300 free Indians and 800 indentured laborers volunteered. The corps under Gandhi's leadership won British admiration; it was mentioned in dispatches, and war medals were awarded to Gandhi and several other members. Gandhi expected the position of the Indians to improve as a result of their war work. He sailed back to India in 1901, where he spent time with leading Indian politician G. K. Gokhale, who was elected to the Imperial Legislative Council in 1901. Gandhi began to practice law and had just settled in Bombay, where he hoped to assist Gokhale's political work, when he was recalled to South Africa. The British Colonial Secretary, Joseph Chamberlain, was to visit Durban and Gandhi was summoned to help put the Indians' case before him.

As a result of the British victory in the Boer War the British were in a position to decide on future policy in South Africa and the Indians hoped for more liberal treatment. However, the British goal was, according to the British High Commissioner for South Africa, Alfred Milner, "a self-governing white Community, supported by *well treated* and *justly governed* black labour from Cape Town to Zambesi,"[8] and Britain's main concern was to secure cooperation from the Boers and to increase English immigration into South Africa. Chamberlain indicated to the Indian delegation he met in Durban that they would have to reach an accommodation with the local white administration, and he did not offer any hope to the Indian delegation in the Transvaal of an improvement in their status. The Asiatic Department in the Transvaal, after failing to block Gandhi's entry into the Transvaal, managed to ensure that he was not allowed to meet Chamberlain for a second time. Gandhi was appalled by the autocratic behaviour of the Asiatic Department, which was in charge of immigration, and decided that he needed to establish himself as a barrister in the Transvaal to be able to do battle with the Department. He began to divide his activities between Johannesburg and Durban, and in 1903 played a leading role in founding and editing the weekly journal *Indian Opinion* based in Durban. He was also beginning to experiment with a new lifestyle and, inspired by reading Ruskin's essay "Unto This Last," decided to set up the Phoenix Community on a farm 14 miles from Durban, where he also printed and edited the new journal.

Gandhi was twice called upon to use his nursing skills in this period. Both cases were revealing of his social and political philosophy and personal courage. There was an outbreak of pneumonic plague in a gold mine near Johannesburg, which infected 23 Indian labourers. Gandhi and some Indian colleagues took responsibility for nursing them and cooperated with the local municipality in moving the Indian community out of their unhealthy location and in preventing the spread of the disease. The second occasion had greater political significance. The Zulu "Rebellion" broke out in 1906. Gandhi maintained his policy of offering support to the government as a loyal citizen of the British Empire, although he says in his biography he had doubts about the extent of real rebellion—the Zulus were refusing to pay a new tax—and his "heart was with the Zulus."[9] His offer to raise an Indian Ambulance Corps to support the Natal Volunteer Defence Force was accepted immediately; when he reached the headquarters he was glad to be assigned to nursing the Zulus, whom the whites were reluctant to tend. This was the closest Gandhi came to associating himself with Africans in South Africa; his focus was on proving Indians should be treated with respect by the whites.

Gandhi launched his first campaign of civil disobedience in 1906 in response to the Transvaal Asiatic Registration Bill (dubbed the Black Act), which required all Indians over eight years old to register and be fingerprinted; those without a registration certificate would be liable to deportation. Gandhi urged defiance at a mass meeting in Johannesburg, and went to London to lobby, with apparent success, for the British Government to veto the bill. Lord Elgin, Secretary of State for the Colonies, accepted the strength of the Indian case, and announced the measure would not be implemented. He knew, however, that Transvaal would achieve Responsible Government in January 1907 and would then be free to pass the act, as indeed it soon did. Gandhi, bitter about Elgin's expedient gesture, formed a Passive Resistance Association, and soon he and over 150 Indians were in jail for refusing to register.

When General Jan Smuts, then Minister responsible for Asian affairs, summoned Gandhi from prison and promised that the act would be repealed if the Indians registered voluntarily, Gandhi accepted the offer in the spirit of trust and compromise he believed appropriate to his strategy of satyagraha. There was bitter opposition from some Indians to Gandhi's compromise (Gandhi was physically attacked when he went to register), and Gandhi's faith in Smuts proved to be misplaced when, after the Indians had registered, the Transvaal government failed to repeal the act. Gandhi led a new campaign of resistance which began with a mass public burning of the registration certificates in August 1908, and then Gandhi and prominent Indians from Natal defied the Act by crossing illegally into Transvaal. Many Indians, including Gandhi, were jailed under harsh conditions. The satyagraha campaign continued with varying degrees of intensity until 1911. Gandhi visited England in 1909 to campaign for support in Britain, where he won official backing from Lord Ampthill, former Governor of Madras, who chaired the British South African Indian Committee, and from unofficial groups, but achieved no tangible results.

On his return Gandhi founded a new community, Tolstoy Farm, 21 miles from Johannesburg, which was given to him by a German architect and which provided a refuge for the families of men imprisoned for civil disobedience. Tolstoy Farm also enabled Gandhi to carry out further experiments in education and nature cure, and provided an example of self-sufficiency and simple living. He had already developed the main tenets of his theory of satyagraha, inspired by both the New Testament and the Gita, but influenced most directly by the writings of the Russian novelist and anarchist, Leo Tolstoy, with whom he corresponded in 1909 and 1910. On his return journey from England in 1909 he also wrote *Hind Swaraj*, the pamphlet in which he decisively rejected Western civilization as a model for India.

The formation of the Union of South Africa with Dominion Status in May 1910 meant that the British Government had no direct role in South African policy-making. Gandhi and Smuts, now Minister of the Interior for South Africa, renewed negotiations on the Immigration Bill for the new Union, Gandhi arguing the Indian position that any racial distinctions in the law were unacceptable. Gandhi was, however, prepared to concede an educational qualification, which would in practice exclude many Indians. Early in 1911 an acceptable settlement was announced, and in 1912 Gokhale, now leader of the Indian National Congress, visited South Africa and also held talks with Smuts. Gokhale was convinced that the Transvaal Black Act and the three-pound poll tax for former indentured labourers in Natal would be repealed. Gandhi was more sceptical and was proved correct: the repealing of the Transvaal Act was a mere technicality since its provisions were reenacted at Union level; and Smuts refused to abolish the Natal poll tax.

The last major satyagraha campaign led by Gandhi in South Africa was, however, sparked by a different issue. A Justice of the

Cape division of the Supreme Court made a ruling in March 1913 that supplemented previous legal decisions that polygamous marriages would not be recognized for purposes of immigration, but declared in addition that now *only* Christian marriages were legal. This ruling, which relegated wives to the status of concubines and invalidated children's inheritance rights, outraged the Indian community. For the first time many women joined in open civil disobedience: the campaign began when a group of 16 women, including Kasturbai, crossed illegally from Natal to Transvaal and then 11 women from Tolstoy Farm repeated the illegal crossing in the other direction. The first group was arrested immediately. The resistance to the ruling also mobilized for the first time the Indian indentured labourers.

The women crossing from the Transvaal, who had not originally been arrested, went on to the Newcastle coal mines and called on the miners to strike. Soon 5,000 were on strike. Gandhi became responsible for looking after them, after the mine owners turned off the water supply in the compound, and marched them into Transvaal and then back again. The authorities refused to arrest them, but eventually transported the miners back to their mines, imprisoned them in a stockade and whipped them when they refused to resume work. This action prompted about 50,000 Indian workers to go on strike, and some were killed when soldiers were sent to put down the resistance. By this stage there were also several thousand Indians in prison, including Gandhi. News of events in South Africa created outrage in India and the British Viceroy publicly criticised the South African government. Gandhi was released from prison in December 1913 and the authorities set up a commission to investigate the Indian grievances. Gandhi was unhappy with the composition of this commission, and was about to boycott it and to launch new civil disobedience when the white South African railway workers went on strike. Instead of stepping up the pressure to harass the government, Gandhi, in accord with his principles of not taking advantage of an opponent's difficulties, abandoned his proposed march. Smuts met with him and lengthy

negotiations ensued, which by 30 June resulted in a formal agreement confirmed by an exchange of letters. Smuts had agreed to
declare Hindu, Muslim and Parsi marriages valid, to enable all
wives from India to join their husbands and allow free Indians to
continue entering South Africa, and to repeal the three-pound poll
tax on former indentured labourers. The concessions to South
African fears were that free movement between South African
provinces in general was banned (more liberal provisions applied
to Cape Colony) and immigration of indentured labourers would
cease in 1920. Most of these measures were incorporated into the
1914 Indian Relief Bill.

Gandhi was now free to return to India. He sailed for England
in July 1914, and gave Smuts as a gift leather sandals which he had
made in prison. Smuts, whose main reaction was relief that he could
concentrate on creating the new state of South Africa, commented:
"The saint has left our shores, I sincerely hope for ever."[10] However, in a graceful tribute to Gandhi Smuts returned the sandals in
1939, writing that he had worn them often, "even though I may feel
that I am not worthy to stand in the shoes of so great a man."[11]

Gandhi in India

Gandhi returned to India in January 1915. He had reached
London just as the First World War broke out and set up an Indian
Ambulance Corps there, primarily to nurse wounded Indian soldiers. When he arrived in India he hoped to work with Gokhale, the
political leader he most admired, but Gokhale died in February
1915. Gandhi applied to join Gokhale's organization, the Servants
of India Society, but members of the society indicated the extent of
their disagreement with his anti-Western and anarchist views. He
did, however, follow Gokhale's advice to spend a year listening and
learning before engaging in public action. He travelled extensively
by train, going third class, and set up an ashram at Sabarmati, near
Ahmedabad. The ashram soon became embroiled in social controversy because Gandhi insisted on admitting a family of untouchables. When Gandhi did take up a political cause, it stemmed

naturally from his South African concerns. He began to tour India early in 1917 to promote national agitation for a speedy end to the system of indentured Indian labour being sent overseas in conditions of near-slavery. The British agreed in principle that indentured labour should end, but were unwilling to end it abruptly. Gandhi persuaded campaigners to call for a deadline of 31 July 1917. The government did then announce an end to emigration of indentured labourers before that date.

Although Gandhi worked with prominent Indian politicians and leaders of Indian society in his campaign to end indentured labour, in his early years in India his concerns were in general remote from those of Indian nationalists. While the pressures of war on Britain were encouraging nationalists to organise and to call for Home Rule, Gandhi was prepared in July 1918 to tour Bihar and Gujarat urging Indian volunteers to fight for the British. The political activities in which he engaged were mostly local, in response to appeals for help from those who were being economically oppressed. Therefore, after becoming involved in local agitation against a customs post in Kathiawad, which was a major inconvenience to local travellers, Gandhi responded in 1917 to a plea from a prosperous peasant to travel to Champaran in Bihar. Here he undertook one of his most famous campaigns in support of the peasants planting indigo against their landlords, and forged his typical approach to this kind of satyagraha. He refused to obey an order from the District Magistrate to leave the area, and legal proceedings against him were dropped on the orders of higher authority. He then proceeded to engage in a lengthy fact finding exercise, travelling among the peasants, and prompted a government inquiry, on which he served. As a result the Bihar legislature abolished the system of indigo planting and reduced rents which had been raised in lieu of indigo production. Gandhi also promoted education, medical care and work among village women. In Champaran Gandhi gathered around him coworkers such as Rajendra Prasad, who remained lifelong associates, gained national publicity and attracted the attention of prominent Indian nationalists like the young Jawaharlal Nehru.

After Champaran Gandhi was called on to lead a campaign in the Kheda district of his home state of Gujarat, where the farmers were protesting against high land revenues and where, after failing to secure a government inquiry, he prompted nonpayment of revenues. In Kheda (Kaira in some English versions) Gandhi worked through the Home Rule League and posed a direct public challenge to the Raj. Before launching this campaign in March 1918 he supported a mill workers' strike against low wages in Ahmedabad, the only time Gandhi took up a specifically industrial issue. He achieved very friendly relations with the mill owners and after 21 days a settlement was agreed on, hastened by Gandhi starting on a fast to strengthen the commitment of the strikers. At Ahmedabad he met Vallabhbhai Patel, who became one of Gandhi's key collaborators and a prominent figure in the Congress Party.

A year later Gandhi launched the first nationwide satyagraha against the British Raj in protest against the provisions of the Rowlatt Bills. These bills were designed to enable the Government of India to curb sedition by measures such as preventive detention and removing the right of appeal for certain crimes. They appeared to be a flagrant breach of Indians' civil liberties and they ran counter to the British Government's promise to move toward Indian self-government. Gandhi appealed unsuccessfully to the Viceroy to refuse his assent to the legislation and prepared for mass civil disobedience, which would entail not only refusal to obey provisions of the Rowlatt Act but also selective disobedience to other laws, for example, the sale of prohibited literature. The campaign was launched with a "hartal," a day of fasting, prayer and processions when shops and businesses were closed down, on 30 March in Delhi and 6 April 1919 throughout the rest of India. The initial mass demonstrations were mostly peaceful (Delhi was an exception) and involved many hundreds officially pledged to civil disobedience and millions of protesters in total. The official British report noted "unprecedented fraternization" among Hindus and

Muslims and women and children took part.[12] The authorities responded with baton charges and in some cases firing on protesters and arrested some satyagraha leaders, while preventing Gandhi himself from visiting Delhi. The initial nonviolence of the protests gave way to riots and the killing of some Indian police and British residents. Gandhi decided to suspend the campaign on 18 April in response to the violence by the protesters, saying that in launching the mass campaign before Indians were ready for nonviolence he had made a "Himalayan miscalculation."[13] The satyagraha did have partial success, since the Rowlatt Act was never implemented and a second Rowlatt Bill was not passed. The Rowlatt Satyagraha was most important, however, as a milestone in relations between nationalist leaders and the British. In the course of the protests General Dyer imposed martial law at Amritsar and ordered the Jallianwala Bagh Massacre, in which soldiers shot into an unarmed crowd including many women and children: 379 were killed and 1,137 wounded. The massacre was a turning point in relations between the Indians and the British.

The British Government made several conciliatory gestures, setting up the Hunter Commission to enquire into the Amritsar massacre and through the Montagu-Chelmsford reforms introducing dual Indian-British rule at the local level. Gandhi himself was still eager to respond to British gestures, but was becoming disillusioned. He was also aware of growing impatience among the younger generation of Indian nationalists at the British Government's failure to take strong measures against General Dyer and with the compromise measures of the Montagu-Chelmsford Reforms. Therefore Gandhi launched a campaign of non-cooperation with the British in September 1920 and the December 1920 session of Congress endorsed total non-cooperation with the British, including a boycott of British goods and nonpayment of taxes. University students left their classrooms and many prominent nationalist leaders, including Motilal amd Jawaharlal Nehru, gave up their law practices to take part in the campaign. A visit by the Prince of Wales in November 1921 prompted an intensification of protests including public burning of imported cloth. Gandhi had promised that totally nonviolent non-cooperation could deliver self-rule within a year. When his promise proved to be over-optimistic he averted pressure for violent rebellion by initiating at the end of 1920 a campaign of nonviolent civil disobedience; Congress vested him with sole authority to direct it. By January 1922 thousands of Indians were in prison, including hundreds of nationalist leaders. Gandhi planned to begin civil disobedience in Bardoli, where he hoped to control the campaign, and then to broaden the mass resistance to other parts of India. But soon after the campaign began in February 1922 a procession in a small village in the United Provinces turned into an attack on 22 local policemen, who were hacked to death as they fled the police station which had been set on fire. Gandhi was deeply shocked and again canceled the national movement of resistance to the British—a decision bitterly opposed by many of the nationalist leaders and Gandhi's closest colleagues, including a bewildered Jawaharlal Nehru. Subbhas Chandra Bose, who later led an armed resistance movement against British rule, became more sceptical about Gandhi's competence as a national leader. The British now felt safe in arresting Gandhi, and he was condemned in March 1922 to six years in prison after a trial for promoting sedition.

After the ending of civil disobedience and Gandhi's imprisonment the movement of non-cooperation lapsed. Many prominent nationalists decided to try to promote the cause of Indian independence by working through the legal and political channels open to them. Gandhi was released early from prison, in 1924, after an operation and serious illness. He turned to promoting his own social goals, in particular the cause of Hindu-Muslim unity. There had been a high level of cooperation between the two communities in the mass resistance between 1919 and 1922, partly because Gandhi had backed a Muslim campaign against the terms imposed by the British after the First World War on the conquered Ottoman Empire and this Khalifat campaign had become intertwined with non-cooperation in 1920–1922. By 1924, however, Gandhi was aware of increasing tension between the two religious communities, and he addressed the question in a major article in *Young India* and undertook a 21-day fast for Hindu-Muslim unity in September that year. Gandhi also supported a campaign on behalf of untouchables at the Hindu temple at Vykom during 1924–1925.

He did, however, maintain a political role in the Indian National Congress and its debates about the goal of complete independence. Congress decided at the end of 1928 to launch a campaign of civil disobedience unless the British granted Dominion status within a year, a goal the newly-elected Labour Government in Britain was willing to accept, but bitterly opposed by the Conservative and Liberal Parties in Parliament, who outvoted the minority Labour Administration on this issue. So in 1930 Gandhi again took responsibility for leading the national struggle; the goal was now total independence for India.

The 1930–1931 independence campaign began on 12 March, when Gandhi led a march from his ashram at Ahmedabad to the sea at Dandi to challenge the government monopoly of salt. When he arrived on 5 April the group of 79 committed to defy the Salt Act had grown to several thousand. After Gandhi and his colleagues had initiated mass civil disobedience by symbolically making salt, defiance of the Salt Act began, in Jawaharlal Nehru's words, "spreading like a prairie fire" throughout India.[14] In addition many officials in the British Administration resigned their posts or promoted the boycott of British cloth, resisters challenged the laws against seditious literature and refused taxes, shops and offices closed down, and the British had soon arrested thousands including hundreds of Congress leaders. Gandhi himself was detained on 5 May 1930. Immediately after his arrest 2,500 volunteers marched on the Dharasana Salt Works north of Bombay, led by the poet Sarojini Naidu, who took Gandhi's place. American journalists Webb Miller and Negley Farson wrote memorable accounts of this nonviolent protest, which was met by brutal beatings by the police.[15]

The British Government held a Round-Table Conference in London in November 1930 with Indian representatives nominated by the Viceroy. Since the Congress Party was not present and its top leadership was in jail the First Round Table Conference made no progress. The British then released Gandhi and other leaders as a conciliatory gesture and Gandhi entered into negotiations with the Viceroy, Lord Irwin. The outcome was the Gandhi-Irwin Pact signed in March 1931. The British agreed to an amnesty for all charged with nonviolent political offences, an end to specific ordinances such as press censorship imposed during the previous year of agitation, and to allow making of salt in some areas. Gandhi agreed to end civil disobedience. Congress was to attend a second Round Table Conference to discuss constitutional change, but no commitment was made to independence or Dominion status. Some of Gandhi's colleagues criticised him for his characteristic refusal to extract the maximum concessions possible.

Gandhi was the Congress delegate to the Second Round Table Conference in London from September to December 1931. His visit was a personal triumph. He was received by the King, the Archbishop of Canterbury and leading political and intellectual figures—only Churchill refused to meet him; he was also warmly welcomed by the people of the East End of London, where he chose to stay, and by the Lancashire mill workers whose jobs his cloth boycott had threatened. Politically, however, Gandhi's visit was a failure. The new National Government in Britain was dominated by Conservatives and the British offered no basis for serious negotiations. Samuel Hoare, the new Secretary of State for India, warned Gandhi that the British would crush any further "rebellion." When Gandhi returned to Bombay at the end of December 1931 he told the welcoming crowds to be prepared to face bullets in the renewed struggle. Within a week Gandhi was in Yeravda jail, the top Congress leadership in prison, Congress and associated organizations proscribed, and severe press censorship imposed; political prisoners were subjected to much harsher conditions. The new Viceroy Lord Willingdon and his officials were determined to end resistance, and although there was widespread civil disobedience in the first four months of 1932, by the end of the year the British seemed to have crushed Congress.

Gandhi did challenge the government effectively in September 1932, but the issue he chose was not central to the independence struggle. Instead Gandhi declared in September that he would fast to the death for the rights of untouchables. Gandhi's real goal was to appeal to the conscience of the Hindu community to eradicate the discrimination suffered by untouchables, but the immediate reason for his fast was the British Government's proposal to create a separate electorate for untouchables in a new constitution being drawn up for India. Gandhi's decision to fast on this issue was contentious: the leader of the untouchables, Dr Bimrao Ambedkar, had attended the Second Round Table Conference and urged separate representation; and the British Prime Minister, Ramsay Macdonald, was willing to offer untouchables a double vote to secure their proper representation. Gandhi, however, was opposed to the basic principle of separate electorates as fundamentally divisive. Other Congress leaders, like Jawaharlal Nehru, criticised Gandhi for choosing an issue not central to the freedom struggle for a major fast. But, as often, Gandhi's priorities were moral and social and concerned with the long term rather than the immediate independence struggle. Once Gandhi had started his fast on September 20 there was a widespread response by Hindus opening up temples and other public places to untouchables, and Hindu leaders engaged in extended negotiations with Ambedkar on altering the provisions for a separate electorate. The outcome was the "Poona Pact," which created reserved seats for untouchables, primary elections by untouchables for an initial list of candidates (to be phased out), but final selection by the whole Hindu community. The British Government hastily studied the terms and publicly endorsed them as Gandhi, suffering from high blood pressure, lay close to death. After ending his "epic fast" Gandhi launched a national campaign to oppose untouchability. He was released from prison after his fast and rearrested twice, and eventually promised not to commit civil disobedience for the period of his sentence if allowed to pursue his campaign on behalf of the untouchables, which took him over 12,000 miles across India in 1933 and 1934.

Gandhi resigned from the Congress Party in October 1934 in order to pursue his own vision of an independent India and in particular to promote a programme of economic independence for the villages by the spread of spinning and rural industries. He also pursued his interests in basic education appropriate to India's peasants and the use of Hindi as the national language, in diet and nature cure and in protesting against a number of Hindu practises, such as the ban on child widows remarrying. Despite his formal withdrawal from Congress, Gandhi continued to use his influence to resolve personal disputes within the top leadership and to support Jawaharlal Nehru or block Subbhas Chandra Bose. When the British offered India a new constitution in 1935, providing for substantial measures of self-government but reserving crucial powers to the British Viceroy and Provincial Governors, Congress engaged in bitter debates over whether to take part in the elections and whether to accept government office. Gandhi played an important role in proposing compromises, which enabled Congress to agree in 1937 to take office in provinces where it had won the elections, provided there was a clear understanding the Governor would not interfere in the Congress administration.

The Second World War and Independence

The outbreak of the Second World War created new policy problems for Congress, in particular how far Indians should be prepared to support Britain. The majority in Congress did believe they should endorse the war against the fascist powers, although Subbhas Chandra Bose—who had resigned from Congress in 1939 after a final clash with Gandhi—formed an Indian fighting force during the war to fight with the Japanese against the British. Indian political leaders were, however, no longer prepared to fight for the British unconditionally and bitterly angry that Britain had taken India into the war without any consultation. Gandhi himself was deeply committed to the Allied side but now also totally committed to a policy of nonviolent resistance should India be invaded by Japan. Nehru and Congress adopted the policy that they would fight with the British only if Britain clarified its commitment to an independent India after the war and if Congress were allowed a voice in a national government of India. The British responded in August 1940 by expanding the Viceroy's Council to include some Indian representatives and creation of a representative War Advisory Council but made no commitments about the future. Congress turned to Gandhi to lead a campaign of nonviolent resistance. Gandhi himself and some Congress leaders did not wish to impede the British war effort directly, so Gandhi chose as the issue the right of free speech to oppose Indian participation in the war. The campaign was launched with prominent individual leaders making seditious speeches followed by larger numbers of volunteers—over 25,000 had been convicted by May 1941.

Japan's entry into the war in December 1941 and its victorious advance early in 1942 created a new urgency for the British to enlist total Indian cooperation. The Viceroy released those recently imprisoned for civil disobedience and the British War Cabinet endorsed a new constitutional plan for India, which was presented to Congress by the leading Labour politician and intellectual, Stafford Cripps. Cripps, who knew and sympathised with some of the Congress leaders, seemed well placed to secure agreement to a plan which promised India Dominion status and specified constitutional procedures for the creation of an independent government. There were three crucial objections to the plan. First, it failed to provide for an immediate Indian national government or for an Indian voice in the actual conduct of the war. Second, it promised Dominion status, which was no longer a satisfactory option for Congress. Third, and for Gandhi this was the most crucial objection, the plan explicitly allowed provinces of India to refuse to join the new constitution of India. This opened up the possibility of the Princely States opting out of a Congress dominated federation; but much more crucially it was seen as a concession to Jinnah's Muslim League, which had begun to gain influence in the 1930s, and appeared to endorse the possible creation of a separate Pakistan. Cripps returned to Britain in April 1942 to report the failure of his mission. Appeals by the Chinese Nationalist leader Chiang Kai-shek and diplomacy by President Roosevelt's envoy failed to create any basis for a compromise between Congress and the British.

Both Congress and the British Government had now reached a point of crisis, as the Japanese armies threatened Indian territory and as anti-British feelings within India intensified. Congress committed itself on 8 August to a campaign of mass civil disobedience unless British rule ended immediately. Gandhi, who framed the call for the British to "Quit India," did not at this stage mean that British troops should leave India to be overrun by Japan (he was now willing to accept the necessity for armed resistance to Japan), but that power should be handed over immediately to an Indian government. Gandhi's plans for nonviolent rebellion envisaged non-payment of taxes, illegal making of salt and only partial non-cooperation, since he did not wish to impede the war effort directly.[16] The British Government responded by imprisoning Gandhi, Nehru and other Congress leaders immediately. Violent protests broke out against their imprisonment including attacks on police stations, courts and railway lines. Subsequently there was a systematic underground campaign of sabotage initiated by radical socialists. The British Government blamed Gandhi for the violent incidents of 1942, a charge he refuted bitterly and at length; in February 1943 he undertook a 21-day fast to demonstrate his innocence. The British refused to release him from prison. Churchill, who had agreed to the Cripps Mission in a time of crisis, publicly expressed his determination in November 1942 to keep hold of India: "I have not become the King's Minister in order to preside over the liquidation of the British Empire."[17] The British forcibly suppressed rebellion in India in 1942 and 1943, and Nehru remained in prison with ten of his Congress colleagues until June 1945.

Gandhi had been released from jail in May 1944 when he was very ill with malaria, but had not been able to secure a meeting with the Viceroy, Lord Wavell, or get permission to see imprisoned Congress leaders. Gandhi then embarked in September 1944 on what most political observers saw as an ill-judged attempt at conciliation with Jinnah, who had remained out of prison during the war and in a position to strengthen his demands for an independent Pakistan. The fact that Gandhi, encouraged by his close colleague Rajagopalachari, was willing to go to meet Jinnah at all, and to consider the possibility of a separate Pakistan under some circumstances, enhanced Jinnah's prestige and weakened the claim of Congress to represent all communal groups within an India that should remain united. Jinnah demonstrated his usual intransigence and Gandhi was unable to persuade him to clarify his conception of Pakistan. When Wavell attempted to move toward constitutional change in India at the Simla Conference of June 1945, by setting up a new Executive Council to represent both Hindus and Muslims, Gandhi remained in the background. Congress representatives were unable to reach agreement with the Muslim League and Jinnah's insistence on nominating all Muslim members of the Council, and on a Muslim right of veto on all issues affecting them, forced Wavell to admit the Council could not be created.

The Labour Government elected in July 1945 with a resounding parliamentary majority was committed to grant Indian independence for reasons of both principle and expediency—the large army still in India was awaiting demobilization. After the charismatic Mountbatten had replaced Wavell, to become the last Viceroy, he persuaded the British Government to bring forward the date of independence from 1948 to August 1947. The central problem in the complex negotiations between July 1945 and July 1947 was how to reconcile the demands of Congress and the Muslim League. Gandhi did play some role in the final negotiations for independence, although he was no longer a central figure in Congress decision-making. He may have influenced Congress's rejection of proposals brought by the British Cabinet Mission in March 1946, and he desperately sought an alternative to partition, such as allowing Jinnah the power to head an interim government, an idea that his political colleagues understandably rejected. It was feared that Gandhi would refuse to accept partition after Congress leaders had reluctantly decided, soon after Mountbatten's arrival in March 1947, to do so; but he gave his support to Mountbatten's proposals when the Congress Party debated them.

Mountbatten sought Gandhi's views and the Congress leaders still came to him to settle their internal quarrels and resolve policy questions. But Gandhi in his final years was most concerned, as he always had been, with the lives of the ordinary people of India and with the creation of a better society within an independent India. In particular he was committed to try to prevent Hindu-Muslim tensions from tearing Indian society apart.

Gandhi expressed public concern as early as February 1946 about the feeling of hatred in India and the outbreak of local communal rioting. In August 1946 Muslim League protests sparked appalling riots in Calcutta which led to 5,000 dead and 15,000 injured, the majority Muslims. Muslims retaliated against Hindus in East Bengal in October, attacking Hindu temples and seizing Hindu women. Gandhi immediately left for the Noakhali district of East Bengal to try, with the help of some of his key aides, to promote communal reconciliation by travelling among the villages of the area. He stayed in one Muslim village for six weeks, often working for 16 or more hours a day, despite his age and frail health. In January 1947 Gandhi started a seven-week walk of over a hundred miles, visiting 47 villages. From Bengal Gandhi went to Bihar, where Hindus had attacked Muslims in revenge for Noakhali, and threatened to fast unless order was restored. After Congress decided to accept partition as inevitable, Gandhi's main concern was to reduce the risk of rioting prompted by partition and the mass migration of both Hindus and Muslims. He stayed in Calcutta, still tense from the earlier massacre, in August 1947. Two weeks after Independence Day on 15 August communal hatreds sparked renewed violence, including an attack on Gandhi himself. He committed himself to a fast on 1 September, which he would not break until he had evidence that the leaders of both communities were committed to keep the peace. His fast did bring about an accord which preserved peace in the city while bloodshed continued elsewhere. Mountbatten estimated that Gandhi achieved more through moral suasion than four armed Divisions might have accomplished by force.[18]

Gandhi intended to travel to the riot-torn Punjab, but had to stop in Delhi, where an influx of refugees ignited communal hatreds. Gandhi undertook his last fast in January 1948 to bring peace to the city. On 30 January, as he walked to his daily prayer meeting, he was shot by Nathuram Godse, member of a conspiracy by young Hindu extremists. He died instantly.

Nehru made a broadcast that evening to the Indian people, "Friends and comrades, the light has gone out of our lives and there is darkness everywhere. I do not know what to tell you and how to say it. Our beloved leader . . . is no more. The light has gone out, I said, and yet I was wrong. . . . For that light represented . . . the living truth, the eternal truths, reminding us of the right path. . . ."[19]

Notes

1. Seal, Anit. *The Emergence of Indian Nationalism.* Cambridge: Cambridge University Press, 1968.

2. Guha, Ranajit, ed. *Subaltern Studies: Writings in South Asian History and Society.* Delhi: Oxford University Press, 1982–1984. Vols. 1–3.

3. Koestler, Arthur. *The Lotus and the Robot.* London: Hutchinson, 1966, and Moore, Barrington, Jr. *The Social Origins of Dictatorship and Democracy.* London: Allen Lane, The Penguin Press 1967. Chap. 6.

4. Gandhi, M. K. *An Autobiography or The Story of My Experiments with Truth.* Harmondsworth, Middlesex: Penguin Books, 1982. 28.

5. Ibid. 39.

6. Ibid. 197.

7. Ibid. 190.

8. Milner Papers, ii. 35–36 (italics in original) cited in Monica Wilson and Leonard Thompson, eds. *The Oxford History of South Africa* Vol. 2. Oxford: Clarendon Press, 1971. 330.

9. Gandhi, *Autobiography*, 287.

10. Hancock, W. K. *Smuts: The Sanguine Years 1870–1919*. Cambridge: Cambridge University Press, 1962. 345.

11. Fischer, Louis. *Gandhi: His Life and Message for the World*. New York: The New American Library, Signet Books, 1954. 48.

12. Bondurant, Joan. *Conquest of Violence: The Gandhian Philosophy of Conflict*. Princeton: Princeton University Press, 76.

13. Gandhi, *Autobiography*, 422.

14. Cited by Bondurant, 94.

15. Miller, Webb. *I Found No Peace: The Journal of a Foreign Correspondent*. New York: Simon and Schuster. Farson is quoted in Bondurant, 96.

16. Brown, Judith M. *Gandhi: Prisoner of Hope*. New Haven: Yale University Press, 338–39.

17. Fischer, *Gandhi*, 135.

18. Brown, *Gandhi: Prisoner of Hope*, 379.

19. Quoted in Akbar, M. J. *Nehru: The Making of India*. Harmondsworth, Middlesex: Penguin Books, 1989. 433.

Chronology of the Life of Mahatma Gandhi

1869	October	Birth of Mohandas Karamchand Gandhi.
1883		Gandhi marries Kasturbai Makanjii.
1885	December	Indian National Congress founded to promote political reform.
1886		Gandhi's father, Karamchand Gandhi, dies.
1888		Gandhi's first son, Harilal, is born.
1888	September	Gandhi travels to London to study law.
1891		Gandhi returns to India after qualifying in bar exams.
1892		Indian Councils Act slightly extends Indian representation on Imperial and Provincial Legislative Councils. Gandhi's second son, Manilal, is born.
1893	May	Gandhi arrives in South Africa and starts legal practice in Durban.
1894	May	Gandhi founds Natal Indian Congress to resist proposals to disenfranchise Indians and proposed poll tax of 25 pounds.
1895		Natal Province imposes 3-pound poll tax on all Indians.

1896		Natal Province disenfranchises Indians who did not already have right to vote. Gandhi briefly visits India; he is attacked by white mob on his return to Durban in December.
1897		Natal Act restricts Indian immigration by requiring property qualifications and knowledge of English. Gandhi's third son, Ramdas, is born.
1899	October	Boer War begins.
1900		Gandhi raises Indian Ambulance Corps to help British at the front. Gandhi's fourth son, Devadas, is born.
1901		British response to work of Indian Ambulance Corps suggests the status of Indians in South Africa will improve. Gandhi returns to India and stays one month with G. K. Gokhale.
1902		Gandhi starts to practice law in Rajkot and then Bombay.
1902	May	Boer War ends. Indians in South Africa summon Gandhi to return to plead their cause to British Colonial Secretary visiting South Africa.
1903		Gandhi founds *Indian Opinion*.
1904		Gandhi sets up Phoenix Settlement near Durban.
1905		Gandhi and family move to Johannesburg in the Transvaal. In India the Indian National Congress supports boycott of English cloth launched in Bengal and backs campaign for Swadeshi (self-sufficiency.)
1906		Zulu Rebellion in Natal; Gandhi leads Indian stretcher bearers to assist British but nurses Zulus.
1906	August	Draft of Transvaal Asiatic Amendments Act (Black Act) requiring registration and fingerprinting of all Indians is published.

1906	September	Meeting in English Theatre, Johannesburg, launches campaign of resistance to registration. Gandhi travels to London to lobby new Liberal Government, which promises not to authorize the legislation.
1907	January	Transvaal achieves status of "responsible government" and is enabled to pass Black Act.
1907	July	Gandhi creates Passive Resistance Association and leads movement refusing to register under Act.
1908	January	Gandhi jailed for 2 months for nonregistration. Smuts offers to repeal Act if Indians register voluntarily. Gandhi agrees to this compromise.
1908	February	Gandhi personally registers despite hostility of fellow Indians. Smuts fails to repeal Act.
1908	August	Gandhi renews resistance campaign with burning of thousands of voluntary registration certificates.
1908	October	Gandhi challenges ban on Indian immigration into Transvaal from Natal. Many, including Gandhi, are arrested trying to cross frontier.
1909		Widespread resistance to registration continues in Transvaal.
1908	July	Gandhi arrives in London to lobby for British support against racial legislation in South Africa.
1908	November	Gandhi writes *Hind Swaraj* on return journey to South Africa.
1910	May	Gandhi founds Tolstoy Farm outside Johannesburg as base for families of those undertaking non-cooperation. Union of South Africa gains Dominion status.
1911		Indian non-cooperation continues. In Gandhi-Smuts talks Smuts provisionally offers to repeal Transvaal Black Act and introduce nondiscriminatory immigration law.

1912	October	Gokhale visits South Africa and Smuts promises him Black Act and poll tax will be repealed.
1913		South African Government refuses to end poll tax.
1913	March	Supreme Court in Cape rules only Christian marriages are legal. Gandhi launches new satyagraha campaign with symbolic crossing of Natal Transvaal border.
1913	October	Indian miners go on strike.
1913	November	Gandhi leads over 2,000 across Transvaal border and is jailed with other leaders. Police fire on Indian demonstrators.
1913	December	50,000 Indian workers are on strike in South Africa, several thousand are in jail. Viceroy of India demands South African Government set up commission of inquiry. Gandhi rejects composition of proposed commission.
1914	January	Gandhi announces march from Durban to court arrest. White railway workers go on strike and Gandhi calls off march. Gandhi and Smuts conduct detailed negotiations.
1914	July	South African Government passes Indian Relief Act ending poll tax and recognizing Indian marriages, but still limiting immigration. Gandhi sails for London.
1914	August	First World War begins.
1915	January	Gandhi arrives in India via London, where he recruits Indian Ambulance Corps of students to work with British Army.
1915	February	Gokhale dies.
1915	May	Gandhi sets up Satyagraha Ashram at Sabarmati, Ahmedabad.
1915	June	King awards Gandhi medal for public service in South Africa.
1916	April	Tilak sets up Home Rule League in Bombay.

1916	September	Annie Besant sets up Home Rule League (to work alongside Tilak's League.)
1916	December	Indian National Congress meets at Lucknow and makes pact with Muslim League.
1917	April	Gandhi leads struggle of peasants in Champaran, Bihar. He is arrested and tried for refusing to leave the area, then released.
1917	June	Government of Bihar sets up official inquiry into peasant grievances. Government of India interns Annie Besant. Many Indian leaders now join Home Rule League.
1917	July	Tilak advocates civil disobedience; Gandhi initiates pledges by 1,000 prepared to defy internment order and launches petition for Home Rule.
1917	August	British Government promises "gradual development of self governing institutions" in India with goal of "responsible government" in Empire.
1917	September	Besant released.
1917	November	Champaran Agrarian Bill reduces burdens on peasants.
1918	February	Gandhi leads Ahmedabad mill workers' strike.
1918	March	Gandhi assists peasants withholding unjust land revenues in Kheda, Gujarat.
1918	July	Gandhi tours India recruiting for British Army.
1918	November	First World War ends.
1919	March	Gandhi lauches satyagraha against Rowlatt Bills, which provided for arbitrary detention.
1919	April	Massacre at Jallianwala Bagh, Amritsar; Gandhi suspends civil disobedience after outbreaks of Indian violence. Gandhi acquires English-language weekly *Young India* and later Gujarati weekly *Navajivan*.

1919	December	Montagu-Chelmsford Reforms introduce "diarchy" at provincial level.
1920	May	Hunter Committee Report reveals General Dyer deliberately initiated Amritsar Massacre.
1920	June	Gandhi accepts leadership of Khalifat (Muslim) movement of non-cooperation.
1920	August	Tilak dies. Non-cooperation movement launched with hartal.
1920	September	Congress endorses non-cooperation, including boycott of new legislative councils and foreign cloth.
1920	December	Gandhi draws up new constitution for Congress which adopts goal of independence for India.
1921	January	Gandhi and Ali brothers tour country advocating non-cooperation. Bonfires of foreign cloth and education boycotts in Bengal and Punjab.
1921	March	Congress launches mass membership drive.
1921	May	Gandhi talks with Viceroy Lord Reading.
1921	July	Ali brothers arrested for calling on Muslims not to serve in British Army.
1921	October	Forty-seven Congress leaders, including Gandhi, endorse call for Indians not to serve in British Army.
1921	November	Intensification of non-cooperation greets visit to India by Prince of Wales; rioting prompts 3-day fast by Gandhi.
1921	December	Government bans Congress Volunteer Corps, arrests C. R. Das and wife in Bengal where thousands court arrest; Congress invests Gandhi with sole direction of planned movement of mass civil disobedience.
1922	January	Gandhi announces tax refusal campaign in Bardoli area, Bombay. Presidency to launch mass civil disobedience.

1922	February	Rioting kills police in Uttar, Pradesh; Gandhi calls off civil disobedience despite bitter opposition from many Congress leaders. 30,000 arrested since December.
1922	March	Gandhi sentenced to 6 years in prison for sedition.
1923	January	C. R. Das and Motilal Nehru launch Swaraj Party to work aginst Raj from within new legislative councils, after Congress in December 1922 had rejected this policy.
1924	January	Gandhi released from prison after appendix operation.
1924	March	Vykom Temple Satyagraha in Travancore on behalf of untouchables is supported but not led by Gandhi.
1924	September	Gandhi goes on 21-day fast for Hindu-Muslim unity after evidence of communal tension.
1924	October	Government raids Swaraj offices and arrests leaders for "terrorism"; Gandhi declares solidarity with Swarajists.
1924	November	Gandhi ends split between Congress and Swaraj Party (the Party to act for Congress in legislative councils).
1925	April	Gandhi visits Vykom temple and persuades authorities to open road to untouchables.
1925	June	C. R. Das dies.
1926	January	Gandhi vows to observe a year of "political silence."
1927	November	British Conservative Government appoints all-white Simon Commission to monitor progress of reforms in India and consider further constitutional changes.
1927	December	Congress decides to boycott Commission and passes Jawaharlal Nehru's resolution calling for complete independence.

1928	February	Bardoli Satyagraha, peasants withholding land revenues from Bombay government, led by Sardar Vallabhbhai Patel and supported by Gandhi in *Young India*. Simon Commission reaches India 23 February; met by hartal and demonstrations.
1928	August	All-Parties Conference at third session endorses Motilal Nehru's "Report" calling for Dominion status and rejecting separate communal electorates. Muslim leader Jinnah opposes it and sets out "14 points" in reply.
1928	October	Simon Commission on second tour of India meets renewed mass protests.
1928	December	Congress debates "Nehru Report." Jawaharlal Nehru and Subbhas Chandra Bose press for goal of complete independence, Gandhi supports Dominion status. Congress agrees to launch mass civil disobedience for complete independence if Dominion status not offered within one year.
1929		Gandhi tours India urging people to prepare for struggle and intensify boycott of foreign cloth.
1929	March	Gandhi lights bonfire of foreign cloth in Calcutta and the government issues a warrant for his arrest. He is released after trial when supporter pays his fine.
1929	April	Bomb is thrown into Legislative Assembly.
1929	May	Labour Government comes to power in Britain.
1929	October	Viceroy Lord Irwin promises Round Table Conference when Simon Report complete.
1929	November	Indian leaders meet and issue Delhi Manifesto demanding that Round Table Conference will discuss implementation of Dominion status.

1929	December	Irwin admits he cannot make this promise. Congress elects Jawaharlal Nehru as President and launches campaign for independence.
1930	February	Congress gives Gandhi sole authority to lead civil disobedience campaign.
1930	March	Salt March against salt tax led by Gandhi.
1930	April	Gandhi reaches Dandi and makes salt. Mass defiance of Salt Laws begins. India-wide non-cooperation civil disobedience and mass arrests.
1930	May	Gandhi is arrested. There are nonviolent raids on Dharasana Salt Works. India-wide non-co-operation, civil disobedience and mass arrests continue.
1930	June	Simon Report published with no mention of Dominion status.
1930	November	First Round Table Conference in London attended by some Indian moderates but without Congress representation.
1931	January	Gandhi and other Congress leaders released.
1931	February	Motilal Nehru dies.
1931	March	Gandhi-Irwin Pact; Congress agrees to attend Second Round Table Conference.
1931	August	Gandhi sails for London. Labour Government in Britain falls and is replaced by Coalition National Government.
1931	September	Round Table Conference begins.
1931	October	British General Election returns National Government.
1931	December	Round Table Conference ends in failure. Gandhi returns to India and Congress decides to resume civil disobedience.
1932	January	Gandhi and other Congress leaders jailed; mass popular resistance leads to 80,000 arrests over 4 months.

1932	August	Communal Award: Government announces separate electorates for Muslims, Sikhs, Christians and untouchables.
1932	September	Gandhi starts "epic fast" against separate electorate for untouchables and discrimination against them. Poona Pact by Indian leaders reaches compromise and is endorsed by British Government. Gandhi ends fast.
1933	February	Gandhi founds weekly *Harijan*.
1933	May	Gandhi starts fast over misbehaviour in his ashram. Government releases him immediately.
1933	July	Gandhi gives Sabarmati Ashram to untouchables and bases himself at Wardha.
1934	April	Gandhi calls off flagging campaign of civil disobedience.
1934	May	Gandhi averts Congress split between advocates of constitutional action and advocates of continued struggle.
1934	October	Gandhi resigns from Congress to continue his own constructive programme and social reforms.
1934	November	Congress wins 45 of 75 seats allocated to Indians in Central Legislative Assembly.
1935	August	Britain passes Government of India Act providing for elected Indian governments in Provinces, but British Governors to retain veto powers.
1937	February	Provincial elections. Congress fights on platform opposed to 1935 Act and wins majority of seats in most Provinces.
1937	July	Congress decides to accept office and form government in 6 Provinces.
1939	January	Gandhi and Subbhas Chandra Bose clash over timing of renewed mass struggle aginst the British; Bose reelected President of Congress.

1939	March	Bose resigns when Congress votes for continued leadership of Gandhi.
1939	September	Second World War breaks out in Europe. Congress votes to support democracies against fascism, but demands British war aims include promise of independence for India before Indians fight for Britain.
1939	October	British refuse to define war aims and appeal to Muslims and Princely States against Congress. Congress refuses to support war.
1939	December	Stafford Cripps visits India unofficially to explore possible moves for greater freedom for India.
1940	May	Churchill replaces Chamberlain as British Prime Minister.
1940	September	Gandhi agrees under pressure to launch individual civil disobedience against Indian involvement in the war.
1940	October	Vinobha Bhave begins individual satyagraha by making a seditious speech.
1940	November	Nehru jailed for 4 years for seditious speech.
1941	May	25,000 now in jail for sedition.
1941	June	Germany attacks USSR.
1941	December	Japan attacks Pearl Harbour. Viceroy's War Cabinet releases Congress leaders.
1942	February	Singapore and then Rangoon fall to Japan.
1942	March	Cripps Mission to India—offers Dominion status after war in return for Indian aid for war effort; but Britian to control defense of India.
1942	April	Cripps returns to Britain having failed to win Indian support for his terms.
1942	August	Congress formally approves Gandhi's Quit India resolution and calls for mass civil disobedience. Gandhi and other leaders arrested. Government suppresses mass protests.

1942	September	Open protests quelled, but underground sabotage continues. Division of Indian prisoners of war formed in Malaya to fight with Japanese to free India.
1943	February	Gandhi fasts 3 weeks in protest against British claims he is responsible for violence of Indian resistance movement.
1943	October	Subbhas Chandra Bose sets up Free India government in Singapore recognized by Japan and Germany and reorganizes Indian National Army to fight with Japanese.
1944	February	Kasturbai dies.
1944	May	Gandhi released from prison after illness.
1944	September	Gandhi-Jinnah talks on Rajagopalachari formula granting possibility of separate Pakistan, but only after creation of independent united India. Jinnah rejects any compromise.
1945	February	Yalta Conference between USA, USSR and UK.
1945	May	Germany surrenders. Coalition Government in Britain replaced by caretaker Conservative Administration.
1945	June	Congress Party leaders released. Viceroy and Indian leaders discuss at Simla Conference postwar constitution for India and interim government. Gandhi refuses to attend as a representative of Congress. Conference breaks down over Jinnah's insistence on equal Muslim-Hindu representation in government and on his right to nominate all Muslims.
1945	July	Labour Government led by Attlee elected in Britain.
1945	August	Potsdam Conference, Hiroshima and Nagasaki are bombed and Japan surrenders. British Government ends ban on Congress Party.
1945	November	Three Indian National Army leaders put on trial. Congress promotes mass protests.

1946	February	Demonstrations in Calcutta over 7-year sentence on INA officer. Mutiny in Indian Navy in Bombay defused by Congress leaders.
1946	March	British Cabinet Mission arrives in India to negotiate basis for Indian independence.
1946	May	Nehru elected President of Congress to succeed Malauna Azad. Cabinet Mission announces proposed 3-tier constitution allowing subfederations of Provinces to decide own constitutions and wide powers to Provinces. Congress reluctantly endorses Plan.
1946	June	Muslim League endorses Plan. Wavell announces Interim Government of 14 in which all the Muslims are League members.
1946	July	Nehru claims publicly that Congress only committed to enter a Constituent Assembly and Jinnah revokes League support for Plan.
1946	August	Jinnah calls for day of Direct Action by Muslims. Demonstrators demanding separate Pakistan provoke communal riots in Calcutta; 5,000 die.
1946	September	British Government sets up Interim Government of India under Nehru drawn solely from Congress. League protests prompt communal riots in Bombay.
1946	October	Wavell brings Muslim League into Interim Government despite its opposition to Cabinet Mission Plan. Muslims in Noakhali, Bengal, kill over 5,000 Hindus, and Hindus in Bihar retaliate against Muslims.
1946	November	Gandhi begins 4-month pilgrimage through Noakhali and Tippera in Bengal to heal communal hatreds. Attlee calls Nehru and Jinnah to London to confer about Constituent Assembly; Jinnah refuses to take part on basis of Cabinet Mission Plan.

1947	February	Attlee announces that Britain will leave India by June 1948 and new Viceroy, Mountbatten will supervise transition to independence.
1947	March	Muslims in Punjab massacre Hindus, and Hindus in Bihar kill Muslims. Gandhi begins journey to Punjab to appeal for calm and stops en route in Bihar to stop bloodshed. Mountbatten arrives in India and calls on Gandhi to meet him in New Delhi; talks with Nehru and Jinnah.
1947	April	After talking with Mountbatten, Gandhi returns to Bihar.
1947	May	Negotiations between Mountbatten, Jinnah and Congress leaders; Nehru calls on Gandhi to return to New Delhi.
1947	June	Mountbatten Plan for India and Pakistan announced, involving partition of Punjab and Bengal and bringing independence forward to August 1947. Gandhi now publicly accepts partition is inevitable and Congress endorses it.
1947	August	India and Pakistan become independent, with Nehru as Prime Minister of India. Gandhi refuses to celebrate independence, spends month in Calcutta trying to defuse communal tensions.
1947	September	Calcutta riots prompt Gandhi to undertake fast to death, and he brings peace to city. Nehru begs Gandhi to come to Punjab where partition has led to mass exodus of refugees and massacres. Gandhi stops off in Delhi where communal riots are creating chaos.
1947	October	Gandhi stays in Delhi touring refugee camps and homes of Muslims and meeting extremist Hindus and Sikhs.

| 1948 | January | Gandhi fasts to bring peace to Delhi; he persuades Congress Government to pay sum owed Pakistan and secures Hindu pledges to respect Muslim rights. Ends fast on 5th day. |
| 1948 | January 30 | Gandhi meets Nehru and Sardar Patel reconcile personal and political differences. He is shot by Hindu fanatic while walking to his daily prayer meeting. |

I. Manuscript and Archival Sources

There are extensive archives available for scholars who wish to undertake research into Gandhi's life and campaigns. Many of these are of course in India, in particular Gandhi's own papers and those of other leading Indian political figures, Congress Party records and files of the British administration up to 1947. The sources in India are indicated below. Researchers particularly interested in Gandhi's South African period may need to consult the governmental files, parliamentary papers and newspaper archives in South Africa. Depending on the focus of the research, they might also find material on the South African campaigns in Indian government archives, private papers (especially of G. K. Gokhale) and newspapers, since publicity and agitation in India about the plight of Indian emigrants to South Africa were an important facet of the movement in South Africa. Since, however, Gandhi's campaigns in both South Africa and India directly or indirectly involved the British Government, and appeals to British public opinion, there are also numerous sources available in the United Kingdom. The official files of the Government of India in the India Office, Cabinet Office papers, Parliamentary Debates and British newspapers are all relevant to understanding the British response to Gandhi. British Colonial Office records contain material relevant to Gandhi in

South Africa. There are also collections of the private papers of many Viceroys of India, British Secretaries of State for India, and British Prime Ministers. These sources are listed in more detail below, as are details of published guides to the collections. In addition there are records in Britain of unofficial supporters of Gandhi's cause, for example the Society of Friends (Quakers).

The India Office Library (since 1982 part of the British Library) in London has extensive materials relating to the Indian independence movement and copies of Indian newspapers and periodicals. It has also been acquiring additional records through exchanges with the Nehru Memorial Museum and Library and the National Archives of India in New Delhi. The library has been systematically transferring its records, including many newspapers, onto microfilm. Copies of microfilm can be bought from the library, and the India Office Library has also sent significant microfilm collections to university libraries in other countries. (For example, in 1975–1976 microfilm of Indian National Congress Reports from 1885–1936 were sent to the University of California, and microfilm of the private papers of several Viceroys of India and of British Government of India Political and Judicial Department files were sent to the University of Queensland.) For further information contact: The British Library, Oriental and India Office Collections, 197 Blackfriars Road, London SE1 8NG.

In addition to the unpublished primary sources there are also numerous government reports, selections from official archives, selections from the Indian freedom movement, and speeches and writings of key protagonists in Gandhi's South African campaigns and the struggle for Indian independence which have been published. These are likely to be available in major university libraries in India, the United Kingdom, the United States, Australia and New Zealand.

Unpublished Sources

a) *Private Papers of Indian Leaders*

M. K. Gandhi Papers, Gandhi Memorial Museum, New Delhi

G. K. Gokhale Papers, National Archives of India, New Delhi

J. Nehru Papers, Nehru Memorial Museum and Library, New Delhi

M. Nehru Papers, Nehru Memorial Museum and Library, New Delhi

Jayaprakash Narayan Papers, Indian Council of World Affairs, Library, Sapru House, New Delhi

Rajendra Prasad Papers, National Archives of India, New Delhi

Papers of other leading Indian political figures are available in either the Nehru Memorial Museum and Library or the National Archives of India. For example, the papers of V.S.S. Sastri, leader of the Servants of India Society founded by Gokhale, can be found in both. The papers of Nirmal Kumar Bose, close to Gandhi in his final years, are in the National Archives of India.

b) Private Papers of British Officials and Political Leaders

Clement Attlee, Bodleian Library, Oxford (Attlee was Prime Minister in 1945–1951. His political papers for 1939–1951 are in the Bodleian)

Stanley Baldwin, University Library, Cambridge (Baldwin was Prime Minister in 1922–1924, 1925–1929 and 1935–1937 and a member of the Coalition National Government in 1931–1934)

Joseph Chamberlain, Birmingham University (Chamberlain visited South Africa as Colonial Secretary after the Boer War)

Winston Churchill, Churchill College, Cambridge (Churchill was Prime Minister in 1940–1945 and an outspoken opponent of Indian independence)

Stafford Cripps, Nuffield College, Oxford (Cripps played a prominent role in negotiations about Indian independence)

Baron Hardinge, University Library, Cambridge (Hardinge was Viceroy of India in 1910–1916 and concerned about the position of Indians in South Africa)

Earl of Halifax, India Office Library, British Library, London (as Lord Irwin he was Viceroy of India in 1926–1931)

Marquess of Linlithgow, India Office Library, British Library, London (Linlithgow was Viceroy of India in 1936–1943)

Ramsay MacDonald, Public Record Office, London (MacDonald was Labour Prime Minister in 1924 and 1929–1931 and Prime Minister of the National Government in 1931–1934)

Lord Mountbatten, India Office Library, British Library, London (Mountbatten was Viceroy of India in 1947. The papers in the India Office are photocopies from papers held in the Broadlands Archives)

Lord Pethick-Lawrence, Trinity College, Cambridge (Pethick-Lawrence was Secretary of State for India in the 1945 Labour Government until April 1947 and sympathiser with Indian independence)

Lord Reading, India Office Library, British Library, London (Reading was Viceroy of India in 1921–1925)

Viscount Templewood, India Office Library, British Library, London (as Samuel Hoare he was Secretary of State for India in the National Government of 1931–1934)

Lord Zetland, India Office Library, British Library, London (Zetland was Secretary of State for India in the Conservative Government in the late 1930s)

Papers are not available for all key figures. There are, for example, no papers for Lord Willingdon's Viceroyalty, 1931–1936, though some of his correspondence is available with the Templewood papers.

For further information see: Royal Historical Society, *A Guide to the Papers of British Cabinet Ministers 1900–1951* compiled by

Cameron Hazlehurst and Christine Woodland. London: Royal Historical Society, 1974.

c) Papers of Unofficial British Supporters of Indian Independence

Horace Alexander, Nehru Memorial Library, New Delhi (Member of Indian Conciliation Group and leading Quaker)

India Conciliation Group Papers, Friends House, London (The Conciliation Group was set up at Gandhi's suggestion at the time of the Second Round Table Conference and was active during the Second World War.)

d) Party and Government Records

In India

All-India Congress Committee Papers, Indian National Congress, Nehru Memorial Museum and Library, New Delhi

Files of the History of the Freedom Movement (Collection of unpublished papers 1919–1947), Ministry of Home Affairs, Political Section, National Archives of India, New Delhi

Proceedings of the Government of India: Home Political Department Files, National Archives of India, New Delhi

For further information see volumes of: National Archives of India. *Guide to the Records of the National Archives of India.* New Delhi: National Archives of India, 1959–.

In the United Kingdom

Colonial Office Records, Public Records Office, London (There are separate sets of files on Cape Colony—1880–1910; Natal—1859–1910; Orange River Colony—1901–1910; Transvaal—1901–1910; Union of South Africa—1910–1914 and Union Acts—1910–1925. See also Secretary of State's Tour: Original

Correspondence 1902–1903 (CO 529) and Register of Correspondence 1902–1903 (CO 638)).

India Office Records, British Library, London. (See Proceedings of the Secretary of State for India in Public and Judicial Department Series (L/P and J) and Files of Private Office (L/PO); see also Central Government Records, Viceroy's Private Office, 1899–1948 (R/3/1), Files relating to Transfer of Power 1942–48 and Files relating to M. K. Gandhi and Civil Disobedience 1922–46. Other papers on the Transfer of Power come under L/P and J/10.)

Cabinet Office Papers, Public Records Office, London

Premier's Office Papers, Public Records Office, London

For more information on these archives see:

Jasbir Singh, A. K. *Gandhi and Civil Disobedience: Documents in the Indian Office Records*. London: Her Majesty's Stationery Office, 1980 (also listed under V).

Public Records Office. *The Records of the Colonial and Dominions Offices*. London: Her Majesty's Stationery Office, 1964.

Moir, M. *A General Guide to the India Office Records*. London: The British Library, 1988.

Public Records Office, *Records of Interest to Social Scientists 1919 to 1939*. Edited by Brenda Swann and Maureen Turnbull. London: Her Majesty's Stationery Office, 1971.

(See also Published Sources (b) for document collections.)

In South Africa

Material relevant to Indian affairs and Gandhi's campaigns can be found in a number of archives: South African National Archives, Pretoria; Cape Archives, Cape Town; and Natal Archives, Pietermaritzburg. The South African National Archives include both the Union Government records and the earlier records from the Transvaal.

Published Sources

a) Gandhi and the Indian Independence Movement

Dalal, C. B. *Gandhi:1915–1948: A Detailed Chronology.* New Delhi: Gandhi Peace Foundation, 1971. 210 (also listed under III. A).

Gandhi, M. K. *The Collected Works of Mahatma Gandhi.* New Delhi: Ministry of Information, Government of India (printed by Navajivan Press, Ahmedabad) 90 vols. 1958–1984. An Index to the Collected Works was published by the Ministry of Information, New Delhi in 1988.

Nehru, J. *Selected Works of Jawaharlal Nehru* (First Series). Vols. 1–15. Ed. M. Chalapathi Rau, H. Y. Sharada Prasad and B. R. Nanda, Delhi: Orient Longman and Nehru Memorial Museum and Library, 1972; *Selected Works of Jawaharlal Nehru* (Second Series). Vols. 1–15. Ed. S. Gopal. New Delhi: Nehru Memorial Museum and Library, 1984.

Das, Durga, ed. *Sardar Patel's Correspondence 1945–50.* Ahmedabad: Navajivan. Vols. 1–10, 1971–1974. Patel's correspondence is organized by theme as well as chronologically. Vol. 2 covers debates about independence and partition and Vol. 4 covers the transfer of power (the communal riots are especially relevant to Gandhi).

Phatak, N. R., ed. *Source Material for a History of the Freedom Movement in India. Mahatma Gandhi.* Bombay: Directorate of Printing and Stationery, Maharashtri State. Vol. 3, Parts 1–4. 1965–1973. These four books in Vol. 3 of the series are focused on Gandhi and cover the periods 1915–1922, 1922–1929, 1929–1931 and 1931–1932. They are based primarily on police and intelligence reports in the Maharashtra State and Government of India archives.

b) British Government Documents: Collections

Gwyer, M., and A. Appadorai. *Speeches and Documents on the Indian Constitution 1921–47.* Bombay, 1957. 2 vols.

Linlithgow, Marquess of. *Speeches and Statements*. New Delhi: Bureau of Public Information. Government of India, 1945.

Mansergh, Nicholas, and E.W.R. Lumby, eds. *The Transfer of Power 1942–7*. London: Her Majesty's Stationery Office. 12 Vols. 1970–1982. (Later volumes are coedited with Penderel Moon.)

c) *British Government Reports and Statements*

The British Government produced numerous reports on various issues relating to India. A few of the more relevant reports are:

The Rowlatt Report. London: HMSO, 1918. Cmd. 9190 (led to the Rowlatt Acts which sparked the Rowlatt satyagraha) (also listed under V).

The Hunter Committee's Report. London: HMSO, 1920. Cmd. 681 (on the Amritsar massacre).

The Simon Commission Report. London: HMSO, 1930. Cmd. 3568–9. (The Simon Commission was appointed in November 1927 from members of both Houses of Parliament to make proposals for India's future.)

Indian Round Table Conference (Second Session) 7th September 1931–lst December 1931. London: HMSO. Cmd. 3997.

Lord Privy Seal's Mission, Statement and Draft Declaration. London: HMSO, 1942. Cmd. 6350. (Report of Cripps Mission)

See Sims, J. M. *A List and Index of Parliamentary Papers Relating to India 1908–1947*. London: Her Majesty's Stationery Office, 1981.

See also Gwyer and Appadorai and Mansergh and Lumby under "Collections."

d) *British Parliamentary Statements and Debates*

Scholars particularly interested in British policy-making on India or in the views of different political parties and individual politicians can consult the volumes of Hansard for relevant years. See *The Parliamentary Debates, House of Commons* and *The Parliamentary Debates. House of Lords.*

e) United States Government Records

The United States government became involved in the status of India for the first time during the Second World War. See:

U.S. Department of State, *Foreign Relations of the United States.* 1941, 1942, 1943. Washington, D.C.: U.S. Government Printing Office, 1951 and 1962.

f) Newspapers and Periodicals

For Gandhi's own periodicals see:

Indian Opinion, Phoenix, South Africa. June 1903–December 1916. Weekly. Available now in the India Office Library and on microfilm. *Young India*, Ahmedabad: Navajivan. 1919–1931. Weekly. Available in a limited edition of 250 copies published by Navajivan 1981 (see also selections from *Young India* listed in Section II); and *Harijan*, Poona: Sastri. 1933–1955. Weekly. Republished as: *Harijan:a Journal of Gandhiism.* New York: Garland Publishing, 1973. Both *Young India* and *Harijan* are also available on microfilm. For the Gandhian movement and materials on Gandhi see *Gandhi Marg* New Delhi: Gandhi Peace Foundation, 1956–1976, and 1977–.

South African newspapers that are relevant to Gandhi's campaigns up to 1914 include the *Natal Mercury* and *Natal Advertiser* (both Durban daily papers) and *The Star* (an evening paper) and *Rand Daily Mail*, both published in Johannesburg. The *Natal Mercury* was one of Natal's leading newspapers and strongly supported restrictive legislation against the Indians in the late 1890s, but printed reports of speeches by the Natal Indian Congress during the early 1900s and by 1913 was supporting Indian demands

for justice. The *Natal Advertiser* was more consistently sympathetic to the Indian cause. The Johannesburg *Star*, a British-owned
newspaper, nevertheless strongly endorsed the restrictive policy of
the Boer republic of Transvaal towards the Indians. It did print
letters by Gandhi during the campaigns of the early 1900s but
remained editorially very hostile to Indian demands at the height
of the nonviolent protests in 1913. The *Rand Daily Mail* reported
quite sympathetically on Indian protests.

There were a large number of Indian newspapers, for example
22 in Delhi alone in 1921, and a wide range of English-language
newspapers and periodicals both British owned and Indian owned.
British-owned papers were sometimes quite sympathetic to
Gandhi; for example, the influential *Times of India* in Bombay
printed articles from Gandhi on the problems of Indians in South
Africa in 1899–1900. However, the *Times of India* was later critical
of the independence movement in India. Leading English-language
newspapers more sympathetic to the independence movement,
which often printed reports of Gandhi's speeches and his letters and
telegrams to the authorities, were: the *Bombay Chronicle* (Bombay), the *Hindu* (Madras), the *Hindustan Times* (New Delhi) and
the *Statesman* (Calcutta). (The *Bombay Chronicle* was especially
close to the Nehrus and is available in the Nehru Memorial Museum
and Library.) Two important periodicals for coverage of Gandhi
were: the *Indian Review*, a Madras monthly founded in 1900 by
G. A. Natesan, the liberal journalist, businessman and friend of
Gokhale, which immediately began to back Gandhi, and the *Modern Review* (Calcutta) founded in 1908, a well-known monthly that
covered Gandhi's campaigns.

The most serious newspapers in Britain that fairly systematically
covered South African and Indian affairs were the establishment
organ *The Times*, London and the liberal *The Manchester Guard-
ian*, Manchester. To gauge the range of political opinion, however,
it might be relevant to consult the conservative *Daily Telegraph*,
the Beaverbrook *Express* and Rothermere *Daily Mail*, the liberal
News Chronicle and the Labour *Daily Herald* for key periods, for

example, Gandhi's 1931 visit to London. In the United States the *New York Times* is the most obvious source; but Gandhi's more dramatic campaigns, especially in the early 1930s when a number of American correspondents covered the independence movement, were widely reported.

II.   Gandhi's Own Writings

Gandhi was a prolific writer. Early in his political career he became an accomplished journalist and pursued his numerous campaigns through the pages of a series of periodicals that he founded and edited. Three of these were English language journals: *Indian Opinion*, founded in South Africa in 1903; *Young India*, 1919–1932, the organ of his earlier activities in India; and its successor *Harijan*, started in 1933. Gandhi's articles were also published in the Gujarati weekly *Navajivan*. He wrote two major books covering the earlier period of his life and several pamphlets, as well as translating a long essay by John Ruskin, *Unto This Last*, and producing a commentary on the *Bhagavad Gita*. Moreover, Gandhi conducted extensive correspondence with governments as well as writing copiously to his friends and associates and answering letters from both well-known and many unknown individuals. In his later years his speeches were carefully recorded, while visitors and colleagues often kept notes of his conversations.

Because of Gandhi's unique status as a religious as well as a political figure, and as the "father of India," his writings and speeches have been frequently republished in India, and there are many selections from his writings on various themes. Since Gandhi's entire output is available in the *Collected Works* (see Section I for details), this Bibliography only lists his more important works and selections of his writings on key themes of interest to the historian or political analyst, or student of Gandhi's moral and social ideas. In addition, selections designed to introduce Gandhi to readers in the West, compiled both during his lifetime and after his death, have been included. The final subsection lists books and articles covering Gandhi's correspondence and conversations with specific individuals of some importance in his life and work.

Gandhi wrote most easily in his own language, Gujarati, and many of his works listed here have been translated from Gujarati into English. Since, however, Gandhi trained as a barrister in London, he was fluent in English, which was also the common language of educated Indians under the British Raj.

II. A. Major Works

1. Gandhi, M. K. *An Autobiography or The Story of My Experiments with Truth*. Harmondsworth, Middlesex: Penguin, 1982. 454. Also published Ahmedabad: Navajivan, 1948. 640.

Gandhi's *Autobiography* was first published in 1927 and 1929 in two volumes and numerous editions are available. It is an invaluable source for his early years, his developing religious views, discovery of nonviolence and growing commitment to an ascetic lifestyle. The autobiography, which is drawn upon by all biographers, covers the period up to 1920, and is particularly relevant for those interested in Gandhi the man and seeker after truth. Readers more interested in Gandhi's political role or thought should look at *Satyagraha in South Africa* and selected writings on relevant topics.

2. _____ . *Satyagraha in South Africa*. Ahmedabad: Navajivan, 1950. 348.

Gandhi's own account of his political experiences in South Africa campaigning against the discriminatory legislation passed by the Natal and Transvaal Provinces, and later by the Union of South Africa, curbing the rights of Indian merchants and labourers. During these campaigns Gandhi developed the theory and strategy of nonviolent resistance (which he called satyagraha, or truth force) and established himself as an important Indian leader. First published in 1928. Translated from Gujarati by V. G. Desai.

3. _____ . *Selected Works of Mahatma Gandhi*. Edited by Shriman Narayan. Ahmedabad: Navajivan, 1968. 6 Volumes: 375; 379–794;471; 464; 514; 555.

The *Selected Works* reprint Gandhi's two books and include some of the most significant of Gandhi's numerous pamphlets, letters, speeches and articles. Volumes 1 and 2 contain his *Autobiography* and Volume 3 *Satyagraha in South Africa*. Volume 4 covers important pamphlets, including *Hind Swaraj*, Gandhi's translation of Ruskin's *Unto This Last* with his own introduction and conclusion, *Discourses on the Gita*, *Constructive Programme* (1941) and *Key to Health* (1942). Volume 5 reprints 100 of Gandhi's letters on key issues and extracts from his correspondence to illustrate his views. Volume 6, Part 1, contains some of Gandhi's speeches on historic occasions, such as the eve of the 1930 Dandi Salt March, at the Second London Round Table Conference in 1931, during the 1942 Quit India campaign and before his last fast in January 1948. Part 2 is composed of selections of Gandhi's writings on a range of topics.

II. B. Individual Works

4. Gandhi, M. K. *Ashram Observances in Action*. Ahmedabad: Navajivan, 1955. 151.

Letters written from prison to Gandhi's Sabarmati Ashram in 1932 include comments on happenings in the Ashram.

5. _____ . *Constructive Programme: Its Meaning and Place*. Ahmedabad: Navajivan, 1948. 31. 2nd edition.

Gandhi's summary, first published in 1941, of the social changes he believed necessary in order to construct complete independence for India "by truthful and nonviolent means," so ensuring a just and self-reliant society. Available also in *Selected Works*, Vol. 4.

6. _____ . *Ethical Religion*. Madras: S. Ganesan, 1922. 64.

Gandhi's views on the need for a framework of morality to guide action, first published as a series of "chapters" in *Indian Opinion* in 1907. Available also in *Selected Works*, Vol. 4.

7. _____ . *From Yeravda Mandir: Ashram Observances*. Ahmedabad: Navajivan, 1945. 67.

Collection of letters written from Yeravda prison in the 1930s to the Sabarmati Ashram, in which Gandhi sets out his guiding ideas and beliefs, and therefore valued as an introduction to his thought. Available also in *Selected Works*, Vol. 4.

8. _____ . *Gokhale—My Political Guru*. Ahmedabad: Navajivan, 1955. 67.

Tribute to leading Indian nationalist and parliamentarian (1866–1915), who formed a close relationship with Gandhi and visited him in South Africa. This booklet brings together Gandhi's various comments on his mentor.

9. _____ . *The Gospel of Selfless Action or The Gita According to Gandhi*. Ahmedabad: Navajivan, 1946. 390. Also available as *Discourses on the Gita*. Ahmedabad: Navajivan, 1987.

The *Bhagavad Gita* is a central text of Hinduism, but Gandhi invested it with his personal interpretation as a commentary on the battle between good and evil in the soul, and as a text on the making of a nonviolent warrior. This translation from Gandhi's Gujarati version includes an introduction and commentary by Mahadev Desai. Gandhi's *Discourses on the Gita* is also available in *Selected Works*, Vol. 4.

10. _____ . *Hind Swaraj or Indian Home Rule*. Ahmedabad: Navajivan, 1962. 110.

Gandhi's 1909 essay represents his early thoughts on the question of Indian independence and marked his rejection of the Western model of development for India. It also criticised advocates of violent revolt. *Hind Swaraj* was originally published in *Indian Opinion* in South Africa. A new edition with introductory comments by Gandhi and a preface by Mahadev Desai was first published in 1939. *Hind Swaraj* is also available in *Selected Works*, Vol. 4 and *Collected Works,* Vol. 10.

11. _____ . "Hindu-Muslim Tension: Its Cause and Cure." *Young India* (29 May 1924). Available also in: *Young India, 1924–1926*. New York: Viking Press, 1927. 21–60.

This six-thousand-word article deals with a topic crucial to Gandhi's vision of a new India and to his constructive programme. Reprinted in *Collected Works*, Vol. 24, pp. 136–57.

12. _____ . *Key to Health*. Ahmedabad: Navajivan, 1948. 83.

This is one of Gandhi's longer pieces, written in 1942 while in detention, on a subject of lifelong interest to him. He was an ardent advocate of a vegetarian diet, nature cure, cleanliness and good sanitation. Translated into English by Sushila Nayyar. Available also in *Selected Works*, Vol. 4.

13. _____ . *Ruskin: Unto This Last: A Paraphrase*. Ahmedabad: Navajivan, 1956. 68

Gandhi's translation of Ruskin's essay "Unto This Last" into Gujarati, translated back into English. Gandhi read Ruskin's essay on a train in South Africa, and it moved him so deeply that he decided to "change my life in accord with the ideals in this book." Gandhi entitled the translation "Sarvodaya" (the welfare of all), a term he then used to denote his idea of communal good and interdependence subject to the moral law. Translated into English from Gujarati by Y. G. Desai. Available also in *Selected Works*, Vol. 4.

II. C. Edited Selections

14. Gandhi, M. K. *All Men Are Brothers*. Edited by Krishna Kripalani. New York: Columbia University Press, 1958. 253. Republished New York: Continuum Publishing Corporation, 1982.

A selection of Gandhi's writings on his life and thought compiled under the auspices of UNESCO. Includes extracts from the *Autobiography* and Gandhi's views on religion, means and ends, nonviolence, international peace and various social and economic issues. A good introduction to Gandhi's ideas.

15. _____. *Basic Education*. Ahmedabad: Navajivan, 1956. 112.

Collection of speeches and writings on Gandhi's views on the need for a practical education and his reasons for rejecting the Western academic model.

16. _____. *Communal Unity*. Edited by B. Kumarappa. Ahmedabad: Navajivan, 1949. 1006.

Gandhi's views on crucial question of Hindu-Muslim cooperation, from his early campaigns in India to his death. The 525 extracts are ordered more or less chronologically, but also by topic. Foreword by Rajendra Prasad.

17. _____. *Delhi Diary: Prayer Speeches from 10. 9. 47 to 30. 1. 48*. Ahmedabad: Navajivan, 1960. 402. Originally published in 1948.

Collection of Gandhi's addresses at his large public prayer meetings in the last few months of his life.

18. _____. *Economic and Industrial Life and Relations*. Ahmedabad: Navajivan, 1959. 3 Vols. 202, 378 and 269.

Gandhi rejected both the Western capitalist model of economic development and the Soviet Communist belief in rapid industrialization and state control. These volumes draw on Gandhi's extensive writings on the village community, small-scale technology, economic self reliance and the concept of "trusteeship" of wealth.

19. _____ . *The Essential Gandhi*. Edited by Louis Fischer. London: Allen and Unwin, 1963. 369.

Selection of Gandhi's writings focused largely on his political views and actions and drawn from all stages of his life. It includes extracts from the *Autobiography* and *Satyagraha in South Africa*. In addition to Gandhi's own works there are supplementary extracts from Mahadev Desai's diaries (Desai was Gandhi's Secretary from 1917 to 1942) and from Fischer's own writings on Gandhi.

20. _____ . *For Pacifists*. Ahmedabad: Navajivan, 1949. 106.

A selection of brief extracts from Gandhi's writings on peace, war and nonviolence designed specifically for pacifists. A more detailed selection is available in *Non-violence in Peace and War* (see below no. 33).

21. _____ . *Freedom's Battle: Being a Comprehensive Collection of Writings and Speeches on the Present Situation*. Madras: Ganesh and Co. Press, 1921. 347.

This collection, introduced by C. Rajagopalachar, is divided into sections on the Khalifat Movement (a Muslim campaign supported by Gandhi), "the Punjab Wrongs" (on the Amritsar Massacre and martial law), Swaraj (self-rule), Hindu-Muslim unity, treatment of the "depressed classes" and of "Indians abroad," plus a substantial section on non-cooperation.

22. _____ . *Gandhi in India: in his own words*. Edited by Martin Green. Hanover, New Hampshire: University Press of New England, 1987. 358.

This selection from Gandhi's works is designed to illustrate Gandhi as an autobiographical writer and therefore gives more weight to his personal, moral and religious views than to his political campaigning. The editor has chosen many of Gandhi's letters together with interviews, speeches, statements and extracts from Gandhi's articles to demonstrate how Gandhi drew on his personal experience and expressed his beliefs. The items are arranged chronologically and cover the period 1920 to 1948. The introduction analyses Gandhi's style of writing and relates it to Indian and English literary traditions, examining why Gandhi strikes many Western readers as naive.

23. _____ . *A Gandhi Reader*. Edited by K. Swaminathan and C. N. Patel. Hyderabad: Orient Longmans, 1988. 172.

These selected writings range from Gandhi's role in Natal to final reflections on "Ahimsa and the Atom Bomb."

24. _____ . *The Gandhi Reader: A Source Book of His Life and Writings*. Edited by Homer A. Jack. Bloomington, Indiana: Indiana University Press, 1956. 532.

Jack includes biographical material as well as selections from Gandhi's own extensive writings. The book is organized to illustrate central historical events and key themes in Gandhi's life.

25. _____ . *Gandhiji's Correspondence with the Government: 1942–1944*. Ahmedabad: Navajivan, 1945. 283. Reprinted 1957.

This collection includes Gandhi's correspondence with Lord Linlithgow and the Government of India before, during and after his 1943 fast. A major section (pp. 93–154) contains Gandhi's reply to the Government of India's critical report "Congress Responsibility for the Disturbances 1942–43."

Letters from Mira Behn (Madeleine Slade), refuting British press accusations that Gandhi was a pro-Japanese Quisling, are appended. A more personal section contains letters between Gandhi and the authorities relating to the illness and death of his wife while he was in prison (pp. 222–65).

26. _____ . *Gandhiji's Correspondence with the Government:1944–1947*. Ahmedabad: Navajivan, 1959. 375.

This volume prints Gandhi's letters during the negotiations that led to independence and to partition of the Indian sub-continent between India and Pakistan. So it is an important source for Gandhi's views on the key issue of Hindu-Muslim relations and his attempts to avoid partition.

27. ———. *In Search of the Supreme.* Edited by V. B. Kher. Ahmedabad: Navajivan, 1961 and 1962. 3 Vols.: 388, 344, 351.

Collection of Gandhi's utterances on morality and religion, reflecting his lifelong concern with spiritual questions and his search for a unifying rather than a divisive approach to religious belief and worship.

28. ———. *India's Case for Swaraj: Being Select Speeches, Writings, Interviews et cetera of Mahatma Gandhi in England and India, September 1931 to January 1932.* Edited by Waman P. Kabadi. Bombay: Yesjanand, 1933. 416. 2nd edition.

Valuable source for Gandhi's statements on the need for Indian independence during his stay in England from September to December 1931, when he attended the Second Round Table Conference, and on his return to India and to prison at the beginning of 1932. (See also no. 32.)

29. ———. *Mahatma Gandhi: His Own Story.* Edited by Charles F. Andrews. London: Allen and Unwin, 1930. 372.

This volume includes excerpts from the *Autobiography*, *Satyagraha in South Africa* and *Hind Swaraj*. It is one of a series edited by Andrews, one of Gandhi's close friends and admirers, designed to introduce Gandhi to the West. (See also C. F. Andrews, ed., *Mahatma Gandhi at Work*, Section IV, and *Mahatma Gandhi's Ideas*, Section IX.)

30. ———. *The Mind of Mahatma Gandhi.* Edited by R. K. Prabhu and U. R. Rao. London: Oxford University Press, 1945. 226.

Selection of brief quotations to illustrate various aspects of Gandhi's thought.

31. _____ . *Moral and Political Writings*. Edited by R. N. Iyer. Oxford: Clarendon Press, 1986 and 1987. 3 Vols. Vol. 1, "Civilization, Politics and Religion," 1986. 625. Vol. 2, "Truth and Nonviolence," 1986. 678. Vol. 3, "Nonviolent Resistance and Social Transformation," 1987. 641.

Ragavan Iyer, who compiled these substantial selections from Gandhi's works, has also written an authoritative analysis of Gandhi's moral and political thought (see Section IX). Iyer has since published a shorter selection: *Gandhi's Essential Writings*. Delhi: Oxford University Press, 1991. 472.

32. _____ . *The Nation's Voice*. Edited by C. Rajagopalachar and J. C. Kumarappa. Ahmedabad: Navajivan, 1932. 340.

Gandhi's speeches in England, focusing primarily on the 1931 Round Table Conference in London, supplemented by narrative by Mahadev Desai. (See also no. 28.)

33. _____ . *Non-violence in Peace and War*. Ahmedabad: Navajivan, 2 Vols. 1942 and 1948. 512, 393.

Selection of speeches and writings drawn principally from Gandhi's weekly journals *Young India* and *Harijan*. Volume 1 includes materials from 1920 to 1942 and begins with Gandhi's article "The Doctrine of the Sword," which asserts his belief that violent resistance is preferable to cowardice, but that the ideal is the nonviolent resistance of the courageous. He therefore urges India to adopt nonviolence not "because she is weak" but in awareness of "her strength and power." In 1942 *Harijan* was banned and Gandhi was sent to jail. Volume 2 covers Gandhi's writings from 1946, when he was again free to write for *Harijan*. It begins with a discussion of the problems of sabotage and secrecy and ends with Gandhi's "Last Will and Testament," his draft for the constitution of a transformed Congress Party written on the day of his death. A condensed version of these two volumes was published in the United States: Thomas Merton, ed. *Gandhi on Non-Violence: Selected Texts from Gandhi's Non-violence in Peace and War.* New York: New Directions, 1965.

34. _____ . *Quit India.* Edited by R. K. Prabhu and U. R. Rao. Bombay: Padma, 1942. 84. Revised and extended edition.

Selection of Gandhi's utterances published at the time of the Quit India campaign, the last major campaign against British rule.

35. _____ . *Sarvodaya: The Welfare of All.* Edited by Bharatan Kumarappa. Ahmedabad: Navajivan. 1958. 215.

Selected writings giving Gandhi's views on the creation of a good society. A shorter compilation of writings on this theme, edited by S. N. Agarwal, was published earlier by Navajivan under the title *Sarvodaya:Its Principles and Programme.* 1951. 61.

36. _____ . *Satyagraha:Nonviolent Resistance.* Ahmedabad: Navajivan, 1958. 404.

Selection of Gandhi's writings and speeches on the important theme of nonviolent struggle, first published in 1951. This 1958 edition was also published in the United States as: M. K. Gandhi, *Non-violent Resistance.* New York: Schocken Books, 1961.

37. _____ . *Selected Writings of Mahatma Gandhi.* Edited by Ronald Duncan. London: Faber and Faber, 1951. 253. Reissued in 1983 as *Writings of Mahatma Gandhi.* London: Fontana.

This selection lays some emphasis on Gandhi's religious as well as his social and political thought. It includes correspondence with Tolstoy and Tagore as well as with British Viceroys of India, and also includes a report on Gandhi's 1922 trial.

38. _____ . *Selections from Gandhi.* Edited by Nirmal Kumar Bose. Ahmedabad: Navajivan, 1957. 320.

Selection of writings and speeches organized under different topics. This is a revised and extended version of the edition first published in 1934 and compiled by a close associate of Gandhi.

39. _____ . *Speeches and Writings of M. K. Gandhi*. Edited by C. F. Andrews. Madras: Natesan, 1927. 848.

This volume is introduced by a 64-page biographical sketch by Charles Andrews, and then covers Gandhi on the South African Indian question, Indians in the colonies, passive resistance, the Champaran campaign, the Rowlatt Bills, the Non-cooperation Movement 1920–1922 and his 1922 trial. It also includes material on his experiences in jail as well as his early speeches in India. Appreciations of Gandhi by other significant figures appear as appendices.

40. _____ . *Teachings of Mahatma Gandhi*. Edited by Jag Parvesh Chander. Lahore: The Indian Printing Works, 1947. 620.

Short extracts arranged alphabetically under a very wide range of headings.

41. _____ . *Untouchability*. Edited by D. R. Parkesh. Lahore: Gandhi Publications League, 1945. 81.

Selection of statements on one of Gandhi's central concerns: ending the extreme poverty and outcast status of the untouchables.

42. _____ . *Women and Social Injustice*. Ahmedabad: Navajivan, 1942. 216. 3rd enlarged edition.

Selection of Gandhi's writings on the legal, social and religious discrimination suffered by women.

43. _____ . *Young India 1919–1922*. Triplicane, Madras: S. Ganesan, 1922. 2 Vols. 1119 (both vols.).

Collection of Gandhi's articles in his weekly paper during the Ahmedabad textile workers' struggle, the civil disobedience against the Rowlatt Bills and the 1920–1922 Non-cooperation

Movement, up to Gandhi's imprisonment. Articles organized by topic.

44. _____ . *Young India 1922–1924*. Triplicane, Madras: S. Ganesan, 1924. 2 Vols. 1256 (both vols.).

Articles from the period of Gandhi's imprisonment.

45. _____ . *Young India 1924–1926*. Triplicane, Madras: S. Ganesan, 1937. 2 Vols. 1357 (both vols.).

Articles from period when the struggle for national independence was in abeyance and Gandhi concentrated on promoting his "constructive programme." The Vykom Temple Satyagraha centred on the rights of untouchables, which Gandhi inspired and supported (but did not lead), took place in this period, and so did Gandhi's three-week fast for Hindu-Muslim unity. Published also by the Viking Press, New York, 1927, under the same title.

II. D. Correspondence and Conversations between Gandhi and Key Individuals

46. Behn, Mira (Madeleine Slade). *Bapu's Letters to Mira (1924–1948)*. Ahmedabad: Navajivan, 1949. 387.

Collection of 386 personal letters (out of a total of 650) treasured by Mira Behn (the daughter of a British admiral who became Gandhi's devoted assistant). The letters are personal rather than political and indicate Gandhi's style of writing to his friends.

47. Chander, Jag Parvesh, ed. *Tagore and Gandhi Argue*. Lahore: Indian Printing Works, 1945. 181.

Collection of articles and letters representing the different views held by Gandhi and by the great Indian poet Rabindranath Tagore on political and economic problems and on non-cooperation.

48. Gracie, David McI. ed. *Gandhi and Charlie, the story of a friendship*. Oxford: Cowley Publications, 1989. 211.

Compilation of letters and writings of Gandhi and Charles Freer Andrews who worked closely with Gandhi in his early campaigns in South Africa and India.

49. Nag, Kalidas, ed. *Tolstoy and Gandhi*. Patna: Pustak Bhandar. 1950. 136.

Tolstoy influenced Gandhi's early thought on nonviolent resistance when he was in South Africa and this book incorporates the correspondence between the two men in this period.

See also: Horace Alexander, *Gandhi Through Western Eyes* (Section III.A).

III.   General Biographies

Gandhi has been the subject of numerous biographies. His death in 1948, the centenary of his birth in 1969 and the making and release of Richard Attenborough's epic film *Gandhi* in 1982–1983 in particular prompted biographies and assessments of Gandhi and reprints of earlier works. The list given here is not intended to be exhaustive. The titles have been chosen to include the most substantial and scholarly biographies by both Indian and Western authors but also to include some of the more popular and widely read accounts of Gandhi's life. In addition this section includes biographies and assessments that appeared in the West at various stages of Gandhi's career, from the 1920s to the 1940s, and influenced views of Gandhi and the Indian independence struggle at the time, and that also prompted serious interest in the theory and practice of nonviolent action in some Western circles. Several of these biographies or memoirs are written by people who worked with Gandhi or met him on a number of occasions. There are also numerous introductory biographical studies and a few of these have been included here. Some of the most important biographies and memoirs in Section A and Section B have been starred. There are also interesting and sometimes critical analyses of Gandhi's life and legacy in Section X.

III. A. Biographies and Memoirs of Gandhi

Books

50. Alexander, Horace. *Gandhi Through Western Eyes*. London: Asia Publishing House, 1968. 218.

Biography written partly to save Gandhi from becoming a "myth rather than a real man of flesh and blood." Alexander was a British Quaker who first spent a week in Gandhi's ashram in 1928, was close to him during the London Round Table Conference in 1931, helped to mediate during the Cabinet Mission in India in 1946, and met Gandhi again in the summers of 1946 and 1947. He therefore gives more weight to the post-1928 period of Gandhi's life and includes material from his experiences in the periods he was with Gandhi. The Appendix includes a selection of letters written by Gandhi to Alexander between 1927 and 1948 on political and personal issues.

51. *Ashe, Geoffrey. *Gandhi*. London: Heinemann, 1968. 404.

One of the more substantial biographies of Gandhi, looking objectively at Gandhi's personality and the development of his mind. Ashe consciously sets out to include details of Gandhi's private life omitted by earlier biographers and to counter the adulation of some biographers, for example, Romain Rolland. He deals sensitively with Gandhi's friendship for Madeleine Slade and other admirers, though he is critical of Gandhi's treatment of his family. The focus is primarily on Gandhi the man rather than the wider political context. Includes bibliography.

52. Bernays, Robert. *"Naked Faquir."* New York: Henry Holt. 1932. 333. First printed London: Gollancz, 1931.

Account by British journalist who worked for five months in India in 1931 as a correspondent for the *News Chronicle* to cover the independence movement. The title is derived from a famous comment by Winston Churchill, who expressed his disgust in early 1931 at the "spectacle of this onetime Inner Temple lawyer, now a seditious fakir, striding half naked up the steps of the Viceroy's palace."

53. Bolton, Glorney. *The Tragedy of Gandhi*. London: Allen and Unwin, 1934. 326.

The author met Gandhi in 1930 and sailed from India to London with the delegates to the Second Round Table Conference in 1931. The book ends with the failure of the Conference and Gandhi's return to jail. Bolton makes clear his dislike of Gandhi's asceticism and praise of poverty, so this is one of the more critical biographies written during Gandhi's lifetime.

54. *Brown, Judith M. *Gandhi: Prisoner of Hope*. New Haven: Yale University Press, 1989. 440.

This is a biography placing Gandhi in his social and political context by the author of two scholarly studies of Gandhi's Indian campaigns. Brown stresses his political tactics and organizational methods, but also explores his religious and social beliefs and his personal life and conflicts. She ends with a brief assessment of his role in independent India. A sympathetic but objective biography by a leading Gandhi scholar.

55. Bush, Catherine. *Mohandas Gandhi*. London: Burke Publishing Co., 1988. 112. Revised edition of 1985 book published in the United States.

Brief and extensively illustrated introductory biography in the series *World Leaders, Past and Present* edited by Arthur M. Schlesinger, Jr. The opening chapter looks at Gandhi's choice of salt as an issue on which to launch the 1930 independence campaign, and the final chapter notes Gandhi's influence on later political figures, especially Martin Luther King.

56. Catlin, George. *In the Path of Mahatma Gandhi*. London: Macdonald, 1948. 332.

Account by political scientist of his journeys and meetings in India in 1947 and some of his conversations with Gandhi. Part 2 (chapters 33–43) provides a brief biography of Gandhi and Part 3 includes discussion of Gandhi's moral precepts.

57. Chandiwala, Brijkrishna. *At the Feet of Bapu*. Ahmedabad: Navajivan, 1954. 345.

Memories of Gandhi by a close associate, with special emphasis on the later period.

58. Dalal, C. B. *Gandhi: 1915–1948: A Detailed Chronology*. New Delhi: Gandhi Peace Foundation, 1971. 210.

59. Erikson, Erik. *Gandhi's Truth: On the Origins of Militant Nonviolence*. New York: W.W. Norton, 1969. 474.

Well-known psychoanalytic examination of Gandhi's early career, with focus on the 1919 Ahmedabad textile workers' struggle.

60. Fischer, Louis. *Gandhi: His Life and Message for the World*. New York: New American Library, 1954. 192.

Lively brief survey of Gandhi's life, ideas and impact by an American journalist who knew him and had written a more substantial biography previously. (See below.)

61. *Fischer, Louis. *The Life of Mahatma Gandhi*. London: Jonathan Cape, 1951. 593. Reissued in paperback. London: Granada, 1983.

Sympathetic, vividly written biography, which includes accounts of the author's two visits to Gandhi and is thoroughly documented. It was the basis for Richard Attenborough's 1982 film *Gandhi*.

62. Fulop-Miller, Rene. *Gandhi, The Holy Man*. London: G. P. Putnam, 1931. 191.

This is the second part of Fulop-Miller, *Lenin and Gandhi*. Putnam, 1927. Translated from the German by F. S. Flint and D. F. Tait.

63. Gray, R. M., and Manilal C. Parekh. *Mahatma Gandhi: An Essay in Appreciation.* London: Student Christian Movement, 1925. 2nd edition. 140.

Brief account of Gandhi's life up to 1924, plus a discussion of the value and effects of non-cooperation and of Gandhi and religion.

64. Hunt, James D. *Gandhi in London.* New Delhi: Promilla and Co., 1978. 264.

Well-researched analysis of Gandhi's five visits to London, which examines his reaction to British culture as a student, his role as a petitioner on behalf of Indians in South Africa in 1906 and 1909, his 1914 visit and his attendance at the 1931 Round Table Conference. Hunt draws on Colonial Office, India Office and Parliamentary papers.

65. Jones, E. Stanley. *Gandhi: Portrayal of a Friend.* London: S.P.C.K. 1984. 208.

Jones was a prominent American missionary in India who became a friend and admirer of Gandhi and wrote about him in the American press.

66. Keer, D. V. *Mahatma Gandhi: Political Saint and Unarmed Prophet.* Bombay: Popular Prakashan, 1973. 819.

Keer approached his task as a biographer of some of Gandhi's contemporaries and opponents with the aim of writing an objective account of Gandhi's life and historical role. He includes discussion of the controversial issue of Gandhi's sexual life "essential to an understanding of his career and of the extraordinary drama of his life." Critical but also sympathetic and very detailed biography.

67. Kripalani, J. B. *Gandhi: His Life and Thought.* New Delhi: Ministry of Information, Government of India, 1970. 508.

Kripalani was one of Gandhi's close associates from the early campaigns in India and an authoritative interpreter of Gandhi's ideas.

68. Kripalani, Krishna. *Gandhi: A Life*. New Delhi: Orient Longmans, 1968. 202.

Biography which gives weight to Gandhi's South African experience and the post-1945 period, but is very slight on the campaigns between 1915 and 1944.

69. Kytle, Calvin. *Gandhi, Soldier of Nonviolence: An Introduction*. Washington, D.C.: Seven Locks Press, 1982. 200.

This book, designed especially for "young adults," concentrates particularly on Gandhi's youth and the formative years in South Africa, which the author thinks have been neglected in books published in the United States. Extensively illustrated. This is a slightly revised version of the book that was published in 1969.

70. Lester, Muriel. *Gandhi: World Citizen*. Allahabad: Kitab Mahal, 1945. 199.

Muriel Lester travelled to India and met Gandhi in 1926 and several times in the 1930s. She was also Gandhi's host in 1931 in London. Part 1 discusses Gandhi's ideas on key themes. Part 2 is a brief biography which draws on Roy Walker's then-unpublished study for material (see no. 85).

71. Maurer, Herrymon. *Great Soul: The Growth of Gandhi*. Garden City, New York: Doubleday, 1949. 128.

Brief and uncritical biography: "an attempt not to evaluate him but to show him and his impact upon the world."

72. Moon, Sir Penderel. *Gandhi and Modern India*. London: English University Press, 1968. 303.

This volume in the Teach Yourself History series sets Gandhi in a political context and examines the reasons for his success.The author had served in the Indian Civil Service and was Secretary to the Governor of the Punjab from 1938 to 1942.

73. Moraes, Frank. *Witness to an Era*. London: Weidenfeld and Nicolson, 1973. 332.

The author first met Gandhi in London in 1931 and later when he was editor of the *Times of Ceylon*. This memoir includes chapters on meeting Gandhi (chapter 3), on the Quit India campaign (chapter 9) and the death of Gandhi (chapter 14).

74. *Nanda, Bal R. *Mahatma Gandhi:A Biography*. London: Allen and Unwin, 1958. 542. Abridged in paperback 1965. Reprinted Oxford University Press, Oxford India Paperbacks, 1989.

This balanced and authoritative biography by an Indian historian examines Gandhi's life and ideas in relation to each other and in their historical context. The author notes that it is important that the image of Gandhi should not become "that of a divinity in the Hindu pantheon," but that of a man "who schooled himself in self-discipline."

75. Owen, Hugh. *Gandhi*. St. Lucia: University of Queensland Press, 1984. 48.

Biography in the Leaders of Asia series. Includes a bibliography, pp. 42–45.

76. *Payne, Robert. *The Life and Death of Mahatma Gandhi*. London: Bodley Head, 1969. 703.

This comprehensive, lively biography aims to get close to Gandhi: "to see him striding vigorously along the dusty roads of South Africa and India . . . to watch the changing expression of the eyes. . . ." Payne gives weight to the early years as a key to the complexities of Gandhi. He also looks in detail at Gandhi's assassination and the conflicts in the Congress Party and assesses evidence of possible police complicity in an assassination plot. Includes a bibliography and a family tree.

77. Polak, H.S.L. *Mahatma Gandhi: The Man, His Mission.* Madras: G. A. Natesan, undated. 200. Ninth edition.

Henry Polak was a Jewish journalist who articled as a solicitor to Gandhi's law firm in Johannesburg and cooperated with Gandhi in his community experiments and political campaigns in South Africa. This is an updated version of Polak's original book (published in 1910), which dealt only with the campaigns in South Africa. This edition covers Gandhi's life up to the 1931 Round Table Conference and includes a detailed chronology up to 29 August 1931.

78. Polak, Henry S. L., H. N. Brailsford and Lord Pethick-Lawrence. *Mahatma Gandhi.* London: Oldham Press, 1949. 320.

Polak (see no. 77) covers the South African years. Brailsford, British socialist and journalist, describes the period 1915–1939; and Pethick-Lawrence, longtime friend of Gandhi and Secretary of State for India in the post-1945 Labour Government, writes about the last phase of Gandhi's life.

79. Prasad, Rajendra. *At the Feet of Mahatma Gandhi.* Bombay: Asia Publishing House, 1961. 335.

Prasad, a lawyer, met Gandhi during the 1917 Champaran campaign and became a close associate and one of Gandhi's key supporters in the leadership of the Congress Party.

See also Prasad's autobiography (no. 116).

80. Rawding, F. W. *Gandhi.* Cambridge: Cambridge University Press, 1980. 48.

Short, well-illustrated introduction to Gandhi in the Cambridge Introductions to the History of Mankind series.

81. Rolland, Romain. *Mahatma Gandhi: The Man Who Became One with the Universal Being.* London: Allen and Unwin, 1924. 159.

Well-known early biography of Gandhi by renowned French novelist and pacifist. It looks briefly at Gandhi's early life and ideas, and in detail at the satyagraha campaigns of 1919–1922, which Rolland describes as "the most powerful movement for 2,000 years." Translated by Catherine Groth.

82. Shirer, William L. *Gandhi. A Memoir*. New York: Simon and Schuster, 1972. 255.

Shirer met Gandhi as a young foreign correspondent for the *Chicago Tribune* in 1931. Most of this book focuses on Shirer's interviews with and impresssions of Gandhi from 1930 to 1931, though it weaves in relevant background information. The last three chapters cover the final campaign for independence, the crises of 1947 and Gandhi's death. Includes impressions of other key figures such as Jinnah, Nehru and Patel.

83. *Tendulkar, D. G. *Mahatma: Life of Mohandas Karamchand Gandhi*. New Delhi: Government of India, 1960–1963. 8 Vols.: 338, 394, 327, 330, 353, 315, 426 and 336.

This is the official biography of Gandhi and a revised edition of the work first published by D. G. Tendulkar and V. K. Jhaven, Bombay, 1951–1954, in 8 volumes. It includes numerous photographs and a bibliography. The volumes cover the following periods: 1 (1869–1920); 2 (1920–1929); 3 (1930–1934); 4 (1934–1938); 5 (1938–1940); 6 (1940–1945); 7 (1945–1947); 8 (1947–1948).

84. Tendulkar, D. G., ed. *Gandhiji: His Life and Work*. Bombay: M. N. Kulkarni, 1944. 501.

Published on Gandhi's 75th birthday, 2 October 1944, to celebrate his life.

85. Walker, Roy. *Sword of Gold: A Life of Mahatma Gandhi*. London: Indian Independence Union, 1945. 200.

Account of Gandhi's life written by a British pacifist committed to stress Gandhi's lifelong struggle to promote truth and nonviolence. The author had not met Gandhi, but draws on the writings of Gandhi himself, Mahadev Desai and other key sources.

86. Watson, Francis. *Talking of Gandhiji: Four Programmes for Radio*. (First broadcast by the British Broadcasting Corporation.) London: Longmans, Green and Co., 1957. 141.

Outlines Gandhi's life through a series of interviews with people who had met or worked with him. Issued as a record by the BBC as *Gandhi: The Man and His Philosophy* in 1983 (BBC Records, REH 466 mono; Casette ZCR 466).

87. Woodcock, George. *Gandhi*. London: Fontana/Collins, 1972. 108.

Sympathetic but objective study of Gandhi's life, thought, achievements and failures in the Fontana Modern Masters series. Woodcock sees Gandhi as "the first of the great activist theoreticians who changed the shape of our world and the form of our thought during the present century."

See also M. K. Gandhi, *An Autobiography* (Section II. A); *Speeches and Writings of M. K. Gandhi*, ed. C. F. Andrews; *The Essential Gandhi*, ed. Louis Fischer; and *The Gandhi Reader*, ed. Homer A. Jack (all in Section II.C).

Articles

88. Brailsford, H. N. "Autobiography." *New Statesman and Nation*, 38 (31 December 1948): 783.

One of a number of reviews prompted by the re-issue of Gandhi's *Autobiography* in 1948.

89. Brown, Judith M. "Makers of the Twentieth Century: M. K. Gandhi." *History Today*, 30 (May 1980): 16–21.

90. Erikson, E. H. "Gandhi's Autobiography: The Leader as a Child." *American Scholar*, 35 (Autumn 1966): 632–46.

91. Hay, S. "The Making of a Late-Victorian Hindu: M. K. Gandhi in London, 1888–1891." *Victorian Studies*, 33 (Autumn 1987): 75–98.

92. Saunders, R. "Mahatma Gandhi Seen Through His Autobiography." *Pacific Affairs*, 4 (31 March 1949): 201–9.

93. Watson, F. "Gandhi And The Viceroys." *History Today*, 8 (February 1958): 88–97.

Watson's article stimulated comments in issues dated March and May–June 1958 (pp. 206, 355 and 431).

III. B. Biographies and Memoirs of Gandhi's Colleagues and Contemporaries

Books

94. Akbar, M. J. *Nehru: The Making of India*. Harmondsworth, Middlesex: Penguin, 1989. 609.

A leading Indian journalist's study of Nehru's role in the struggle for independence and the years in office. Akbar examines in detail Jawaharlal Nehru's crucial relationship with Mahatma Gandhi.

95. Ahluwalia, B. K., and Shashi Ahluwalia. *Tagore and Gandhi. (The Tagore Gandhi Controversy)*. New Delhi: Pankay Publishers, 1981. 131.

A survey of the friendship between Gandhi and the great Indian poet and their philosophical and political disagreements. (See also correspondence in Chander, ed., Section II.D.)

96. Behn, Mira. (Madeleine Slade). *The Spirit's Pilgrimage*. London: Longmans, 1960. 315.

Autobiography of one of Gandhi's closest associates between 1925 and 1948. The early pages recount her upbringing as the daughter of an English naval officer and her conversion to Gandhi's ideas after reading Rolland, but the bulk of the book deals with her life with Gandhi. The book contains many personal details of ashram life as well as accounts of major political events. (See also her letters to and from Gandhi, Section II.D.)

97. Birla, Ghanshyam D. *In The Shadow Of The Mahatma: A Personal Memoir*. Bombay: Orient Longmans, 1953. 337.

Birla was a rich merchant who first met Gandhi in 1916 and remained one of his friends and financial benefactors for the rest of Gandhi's life.

98. Bose, Mihir. *The Lost Hero: A Biography of Subbhas Bose*. London: Quartet Books, 1982. 318.

Subbhas Chandra Bose was a leading Congress activist, who broke with Gandhi and Congress in 1939 and became an advocate of violent rebellion. He escaped to Burma in 1941, and began to organize among Indian prisoners of war, first in Europe and then in Asia, where he raised an Indian National Army to fight with Japan against the British in order to liberate India.

99. *Bose, Nirmal Kumar. *My Days with Gandhi*, Calcutta: Nishana, 1953. 311. Bombay: Orient Longmans, 1974. 270.

N. K. Bose was secretary, Bengali interpreter and helper to Gandhi in his last years, and describes Gandhi's ashram in East Bengal in 1946–1947, and his struggle against communal bloodshed in Noakhali, Bihar and Calcutta in that period. Bose includes his own considered assessments of Gandhi's character. One of the most important sources on this period of Gandhi's life. Bose could not initially find a publisher in India because he revealed that Gandhi tested his chastity in this period by sleeping with naked young women.

100. Brockway, Fenner. *Inside The Left: Thirty Years of Platform, Press, Prison and Parliament*. London: Allen and Unwin, 1942. 352.

Autobiography of socialist, peace activist and ardent campaigner against colonialism, who was Secretary of the British

Committee of the Indian National Congress after the First World War until Gandhi prohibited propaganda by outside sympathisers in 1920.

101. Chaturvedi, Benarsidas, and Marjorie Sykes. *Charles Freer Andrews*. London: Allen and Unwin, 1949. 334.

This biography covers Andrews' collaboration with Gandhi in South Africa (1914), in India (1918–1924) and his later role in England promoting Gandhi's aims and ideas. It also deals with Andrews' work on behalf of indentured labourers in many parts of the world. The foreword is by Gandhi himself. See also Hoyland (no. 108) and Tinker (no. 117).

102. Chaudhury, P. C. Roy. *Gandhi and His Contemporaries*. New Delhi: Sterling Publishing, 1972. Revised edition 1986.

Survey of many of Gandhi's aides and political collaborators.

103. Copley, A.R.H. *The Political Career of C. Rajagolpalachari: A Moralist in Politics 1937–1954*. New Delhi: Macmillan, 1978. 337.

Scholarly account of the Madras lawyer who started working closely with Gandhi in 1919 and became a leading Congress Party politician supporting Gandhi's ideas. He diverged from Gandhi in supporting compromise with the British in the Second World War, but influenced Gandhi in 1944 to talk with Jinnah about the future status of Muslims in an independent India.

104. Ghosh, Sudhir. *Gandhi's Emissary*. London: Cresset Press, 1967. 351.

Part 1 of this book is the inside story of the 1945–1947 negotiations with the British Government by the man Gandhi chose to act as his emissary in these negotiations. It includes information about secret meetings with Cripps and Pethick-Lawrence to try to preserve a united India.

105. Gopal, Sarvepalli, ed. *Jawaharlal Nehru: An Anthology*.
     Delhi: Oxford University Press, 1980. 662.

Section 3 of this anthology of Nehru's speeches and writings is
on Gandhi (pp. 97–118). It begins with Nehru's 1928 letter to
Gandhi asking why Gandhi was not taking part in the pressure for
independence, and includes Nehru's speeches as Prime Minister of
India at the time of Gandhi's death and at the immersion of Gandhi's
ashes.

106. Gopal, Sarvepalli. *Jawaharlal Nehru. A Biography*. London:
     Cape, 1975–1984, 3 vols. Abridged edition. Oxford: Oxford
     University Press, 1988. 503.

This authoritative biography spans the whole of Nehru's career
to 1964, so only Vol. 1 (or Part 1 of the abridged edition), covering
the period 1889–1947, deals at length with Nehru's relations with
Gandhi.

107. Hogg, Dorothy. *Memories for Tomorrow*. London: Regency
     Press, 1981.

Memoir of author's work with Gandhi in the 1930s and 1940s.

108. Hoyland, John S. *C. F. Andrews: Minister of Reconciliation*.
     London: Allinson and Co., 1940. 171.

Affectionate tribute to Andrews and his work, which includes a
chapter on satyagraha and Gandhi's campaigns in India from 1919
to 1932, and discusses Gandhi's visit to the Quaker centre at
Woodbroke, Birmingham, in 1931. See also nos. 101 and 117.

109. Kripalani, K. R. *Gandhi, Tagore and Nehru*. Bombay: Hind
     Kitab, 1949. 141.

110. McPherson, Kenneth. *Jinnah*. St. Lucia: University of
     Queensland Press, 1980. 35.

Booklet in Leaders of Asia series on the man responsible for the
creation of Pakistan and one of Gandhi's most intransigent adver-
saries. See also Wolpert (no. 120).

111. Morton, Eleanor. *Women Behind Mahatma Gandhi*. Bombay: Jaico Publishing House, 1961. 311.

Morton devotes several chapters to Kasturbai, Gandhi's wife, and also writes about his mother, Putlibai. She also discusses the role of Mirabehn (Madeleine Slade), the poet Sarojini Naidu, Millie Graham Polak, Annie Besant and Lady Mountbatten.

112. Nanda, B. R., P. C. Joshi and Raj Krishna. *Gandhi and Nehru*. Delhi: Oxford University Press, 1979. 67.

This booklet contains three articles arising out of an academic symposium. Nanda compares the personalities and politics of Gandhi and Nehru, Joshi writes on "Gandhi and Nehru: The Challenge of a New Society" and Krishna discusses "The Nehru-Gandhi Polarity and Economic Policy."

113. Nanda, B. R. *Gokhale, Gandhi and Nehrus: Studies in Indian Nationalism*. London: Allen and Unwin, 1974. 203.

Nanda has written substantial biographies of both Gandhi and Gokhale, the early parliamentary leader of the Indian nationalists and Gandhi's mentor. Here he engages in a comparative study.

114. Nehru, Jawaharlal. *Jawaharlal Nehru, An Autobiography: With Musings on Recent Events*. London: John Lane, 1942. 623. First published 1936.

Nehru's autobiography, written in prison in 1934–1935, includes his impressions of Gandhi. In particular, Chapter 7, "The Coming of Gandhiji," covers the 1919 noncooperation campaign and Chapter 18, "My Father and Gandhiji," describes a visit to Gandhi in prison. An abridged version was published as *Towards Freedom: The Autobiography of Jawaharlal Nehru*. New York: John Day, 1941. 440 and Boston: Beacon Press, 1958.

115. Patel, I. J. *Sardar Vallabhbhai Patel*. New Delhi: Ministry of Information, Government of India, 1965. 175.

Biography in the Builders of Modern India series of the Ahmedabad lawyer who was one of Gandhi's key aides in the early satyagraha campaigns in India. Later he became a major figure in Congress, and he was Minister of Home Affairs after Independence. Chapter 3, "Training at the Hands of Gandhiji," focuses on Patel's links to Gandhi up to Independence. See also Tahmankar (no. 119).

116. Prasad, Rajendra. *Autobiography*. Bombay: Asia Publishing House, 1957. 624.

Prasad was a lawyer from Bihar who worked with Gandhi in Champaran in 1917 and was later a leading figure in the Congress Party and became President of independent India.

117. Tinker, Hugh. *The Ordeal of Love: C. F. Andrews and India*. Delhi: Oxford University Press, 1979. 334.

Scholarly biography of a man who, like "his great friend Gandhi," has been revered in India and treated as "a superman." See also Chaturvedi (no. 101) and Hoyland (no. 108).

118. Scarfe, Allan and Wendy. *JP: His Biography*. Delhi: Orient Longman, 1975. 462.

Jayaprakash Narayan was active in the freedom struggle from 1921. He became a Marxist and in the 1940s favoured violent resistance to British rule. But he always had close ties to Gandhi, became converted to Gandhi's ideas, and after 1948 became a political leader of the Gandhian movement.

119. Tahmankar, D. V. *Sardar Patel*. London: Allen and Unwin, 1970. 299.

Substantial biography of Gandhi's lieutenant in the 1920s and Congress leader and power broker in the run-up to Independence. See also Patel (no. 115).

120. Wolpert, Stanley A. *Jinnah of Pakistan*. Oxford: Oxford University Press, 1984. 421. See also McPherson (no. 110).

IV. Gandhi's Early Years and the South African Campaigns: 1869–1914

Books

121. Andrews, C. F., ed. *Mahatma Gandhi at Work: His Own Story Continued*. London: Allen and Unwin, 1931. 407.

An account of Gandhi's struggle in the Transvaal in his own words, plus an account by Andrews himself of "The Famous March," chapter 20. This is part of the series *Mahatma Gandhi: His Own Story* (see no. 29).

122. Calpin, G. H. *Indians in South Africa*. Pietermaritzburg: Shuter and Shorter, 1949. 310.

History covering period from late nineteenth century to 1949.

123. Devanesan, Chandra D. S. *The Making of the Mahatma*. New Delhi: Orient Longman, 1969. 632.

A very thorough study, based on a thesis for Harvard University, of the first 40 years of Gandhi's life, which explores the varied cultural influences on Gandhi in his Kathiawad childhood. Later sections examine Gandhi as a "Late Victorian" in London and explore the birth of a fighter in South Africa. The author also analyses *Hind Swaraj* as the "Manifesto of the Gandhian Revolution."

124. Doke, Joseph J. *M. K. Gandhi: An Indian Patriot in South Africa*. London: London Indian Chronicle, 1909. 97. Republished, New Delhi: Ministry of Information, Government of India, 1967. 116.

The author of this first account of Gandhi was a Baptist Minister in South Africa who backed Gandhi's campaign for Indian rights.

125. Gandhi, Prabhudas. *My Childhood with Gandhi*. Ahmedabad: Navajivan, 1957. 212.

Memoir by Gandhi's great-nephew of childhood in South Africa. It includes his perspective on the Phoenix Settlement, the move to Tolstoy Farm and details on the 1913 satyagraha campaign. The author also gives his views on Gandhi's theory of education and comments upon Gokhale's visit.

126. Hancock, W. K. *Smuts: The Sanguine Years 1870–1919*. Cambridge: Cambridge University Press, 1962. 619.

This study of Smuts includes an examination of his handling of the satyagraha campaigns and his personal negotiations with Gandhi (pp. 321–47).

127. Huttenback, Robert A. *Gandhi in South Africa: British Imperialism and the Indian Question, 1860–1914*. Ithaca, New York: Cornell University Press, 1971. 368.

Thoroughly researched analysis of Gandhi's role in the context of British policy and South African politics, using both British and South African official sources.

128. Palmer, Mabel. *The History of the Indians in Natal*. Cape Town: Oxford University Press, 1957. 197.

129. Polak, Millie Graham. *Mr Gandhi, The Man*. London: George Allen, 1931. 186.

Mrs. Polak joined her husband in Gandhi's Johannesburg household, and this book draws on her personal memories of Gandhi's years in South Africa.

130. Pyarelal [Nair]. *Mahatma Gandhi: The Early Phase*. Vol. 1. Ahmedabad: Navajivan, 1965. 854.

This is the first volume in a major study by one of Gandhi's secretaries of the early years. This volume ends in June 1896 and so includes the initial campaigns in Natal.

131. ———. *Mahatma Gandhi: The Discovery of Satyagraha— On The Threshhold*. Vol. 2. Bombay: 1980.

132. Smuts, J. C. *Selections from the Smuts Papers*. Edited by W. K. Hancock and Jean van den Poel. Cambridge: Cambridge University Press, 1966–1973. 7 vols.

Volume 2 has some documents relevant to Gandhi and the position of Indians in South Africa.

133. Swan, Maureen. *Gandhi: The South African Experience*. Johannesburg: Ravan Press, 1985. 310.

The author examines the background of "merchant politics" between 1895 and 1906 and then analyses the stages of "passive resistance" between 1907 and 1914.

See also: M. K. Gandhi, *An Autobiography* and *Satyagraha in South Africa* (Section II. A); James D. Hunt, *Gandhi in London*, H.S.L. Polak, *Mahatma Gandhi: The Man and his Mission*, and D. G. Tendulkar, *Mahatma*, Vol. 1 (Section III. A). All the substantial biographies cover Gandhi's youth and his work in South Africa, though the South African period is not always covered in much depth.

Articles

134. "British Indians in South Africa." *Outlook* 97 (4 March 1911): 486–87.

135. Hotz, Louis. "Gandhi's Jewish Associations." *Jewish Affairs* 24, 5 (May 1969): 6–10.

136. Hunt, James D. "Gandhi in South Africa," 61–79, in John Hick and Lamont C. Hempel, eds. *Gandhi's Significance for Today*. Basinstoke: Macmillan, 1989. 275.

Hunt's article includes a bibliography.

137. Huttenback, R. A. "Some Fruits of Victorian Imperialism: Gandhi and the Indian Question in Natal, 1893–99." *Victorian Studies*, 11 (December 1967): 153–80.

138. Murray, Gilbert. "The Soul as It Is, and How to Deal with It." *Hibbert Journal* 16, 2 (January 1918): 191–205.

Murray, a well-known English scholar with liberal political views, met Gandhi in 1914 and here assesses Gandhi's frugal lifestyle and his struggle in South Africa.

139. Power, P. F. "Gandhi in South Africa." *Journal of Modern African Studies* 7 (October 1969): 441–50.

140. Rechlin, S. A. "Some Jewish Associations with Mahatma Gandhi." *Jewish Affairs* 15, 12 (December 1960): 4–7.

141. Switzer, L. "Gandhi in South Africa: the Ambiguities of Satyagraha." *Journal of Ethnic Studies* 14 (Spring 1986): 122–28.

V. Gandhi's Indian Campaigns: 1915–1929

Books

142. Bose, Subbhas Chandra. *The Indian Struggle 1920–1942*. New York: Asia Publishing House, 1964. 476.

   Account by the prominent Indian nationalist who broke with Congress in 1939 and in 1943 became leader of the Indian National Army created to fight against the British.

143. Brown, Judith M. *Gandhi's Rise to Power: Indian Politics 1915–1922*. Cambridge: Cambridge University Press, 1972. 382.

   Scholarly study of Gandhi's role in Indian nationalist politics in this period. Brown covers satyagraha in Champaran, Kaira (often cited as "Kheda") and Ahmedabad; the Rowlatt Satyagraha, the Khalifat Movement and the Non-cooperation campaign, 1920–1922.

144. Chandra, Bipan, et al. *India's Struggle for Independence: 1857–1947*. Harmondsworth, Middlesex: Penguin, 1989. 600.

   This informative historical survey includes a number of chapters specifically on Gandhi's campaigns and the national campaigns for independence which he led, as well as relevant material on other aspects of the struggle for independence. Chapters 14–21 cover the period 1915 to 1929: Chapter 14 summarises Gandhi's early career and the Champaran, Kheda and Ahmedabad campaigns; Chapter 15 covers the 1920–1922 Non-cooperation Movement; Chapter 18 the Vykom Satyagraha on behalf of the rights of untouchables; Chapter 19 the disputes in Congress in the period 1922 to 1927 and Gandhi's constructive programme; and Chapter 21 the buildup in the years 1927 to 1929 to civil disobedience.

145. Desai, Mahadev H. *Day to Day with Gandhi*. 4 Vols. Varanasi: Sarva Seva Sangh Prakashan, 1968–1969. 400, 400, 400, 388.

Desai was Gandhi's chief secretary from 1917 until he died in 1942, and was so close to Gandhi that he has been described as "both his hands." These volumes reproduce Desai's diaries for the periods November 1917 to March 1919 (Vol. 1), April 1919 to October 1920 (Vol. 2), October 1920 to January 1924 (Vol. 3) and January 1924 to November 1924 (Vol. 4).

146. _____ . *The Epic of Travancore*. Ahmedabad: Navajivan, 1937. 251.

An account of the 1924 to 1925 Vykom Temple Road struggle on behalf of the untouchables, led by associates of Gandhi, together with selections from Gandhi's writings.

147. _____ . *A Righteous Struggle: A Chronicle of the Ahmed-abad Textile Labourers' Fight for Justice*. Ahmedabad: Nava-jivan, 1951. 97.

Ahmedabad was one of Gandhi's more important campaigns on specific issues and the only one on behalf of industrial workers. Desai gives an account from Gandhi's perspective.

148. _____ . *The Story of Bardoli: Being a history of the Bardoli satyagraha of 1928 and its sequel*. Ahmedabad: Navajivan, 1929. 363.

Account of campaign by peasants against tax assessments on land led by Sardar Patel. Includes Gandhi's speeches when he visited Bardoli and documents relating to the Enquiry Committee set up by the Government.

149. Furneaux, Rupert. *Massacre at Amritsar*. London: Allen and Unwin, 1963. 183.

Account of the infamous Jallianwala Bagh Massacre at Amritsar ordered by General Dyer on 13 April 1919 when a crowd gathered to protest against the Rowlatt Bills as part of a nationwide campaign. The massacre and subsequent martial law in the Punjab were a turning point in the independence struggle.

150. Gopal, Ram. *How India Struggled for Freedom: A Political History*. Bombay: Book Centre, 1967. 469.

This history covers the nonviolent campaign in Bengal in 1903 to 1906 and the developing struggle for independence to the Quit India Movement during the Second World War.

151. Gopal, S. *The Viceroyalty of Lord Irwin: 1926–31*. London: Oxford University Press, 1957. 152.

Analysis of British policy during an important phase of the Indian independence struggle. Includes material on the 1928 Bardoli campaign.

152. Hardiman, David. *Peasant Nationalism of Gujarat: Kheda District 1917–1934*. New Delhi: Oxford University Press, 1981. 309.

Scholarly account of 1918 Kheda satyagraha for reduction of land revenues organized by Vallabhbhai Patel with Gandhi's support. The book also covers later violent protests by the poorer peasants in the district.

153. Jasbir Singh, A. K., ed. *Gandhi and Civil Disobedience: Documents in the Indian Office Records 1922–1946*. London: Her Majesty's Stationery Office, 1980. 62.

154. Judd, Denis. *Lord Reading: Rufus Isaacs, First Marquess of Reading, Lord Chief Justice and Viceroy of India.* London: Weidenfeld and Nicolson, 1982. 316.

Chapter 14 covers the period 1921–1926 when Lord Reading was Viceroy and notes Reading's impressions of Gandhi in their conversation in 1921 and the scope of their May 1921 talks. Chapter 17 touches briefly on Reading's advice about the Second Round Table Conference in November 1931 (pp. 270–71).

155. Krishnadas. *Seven Months with Mahatma Gandhi: Being an Inside View of the Non-Cooperation Movement (1921–1922).* Vol. 1. Triplicane, Madras: S. Ganesan, 1928. 449. Vol. 2. Dighwara, Bihar: Rambinode Sinha, 1928. 505.

156. Kumar, Ravinder, ed. *Essays on Gandhian Politics: The Rowlatt Satyagraha.* Oxford: Clarendon Press, 1971. 347.

Essays analysing the influences on Gandhi's thought, Gandhi in 1919, preparatory organization for the Rowlatt satyagraha, its development in the Central Provinces and Bihar and its spread to others parts of India. The Government of India's reactions to the first non-cooperation movement are also examined.

157. Low, D. A., ed. *Congress and the Raj: Faces of Indian Struggle 1917–47.* London: Arnold-Heinemann, 1977. 513.

158. Mayer, Peter, ed. *The Pacifist Conscience.* Harmondsworth, Middlesex: Penguin, 1966. 447.

Collection including brief summary of Gandhi's approach to civil disobedience, an account of Gandhi's 1922 arrest and trial and the text of Gandhi's Statement and the Judgement (pp. 203–216). Mayer also includes an important article from *Young India* in August 1920, "The Doctrine of the Sword."

159. Misra, B. B., ed. *Select Documents on Mahatma Gandhi's Movement in Champaran 1917–18,* Patna: Government of Bihar, 1963.

160. Montagu, Edwin S. *An Indian Diary*. London: Heinemann, 1930. 410. Edited by Venetia Montagu.

Montagu was a liberaly-minded Secretary of State for India from 1917 to 1922 and promoted the 1919 Montagu-Chelmsford Reforms. He met Gandhi during his 1917 visit to India.

161. Nehru, Jawarharlal. *The Discovery of India*. New York: John Day, 1946. 595.

Nehru includes an extended section on the Indian National Congress and British reactions to it.

162. Pande, B. N., ed. *A Centenary History of the Indian National Congress*. 3 Vols. New Delhi: 1985.

Volume 2 covers the period 1919 to 1936 and the role played by Congress in the independence struggle.

163. Prasad, Rajendra. *Satyagraha in Champaran*. Ahmedabad: Navajivan, 1949. 224.

Gandhi's first campaign in India was to lead the peasants of Champaran in a struggle against the local landlords. This detailed account was first written in 1918–1919, and first published in English in 1928. This is a revised edition.

164. Ram, Raja. *The Jallianwala Bagh Massacre: A Premeditated Plan*. Chandigarh: Punjab University Publication Bureau, 1969. 208.

An interpretation of the causes of the notorious Amritsar Massacre, which significantly strengthened the demand for full independence from Britain. (See also no. 149.)

165. Ravindran, T. K. *Vaikom Satyagraha and Gandhi*. Trivandrum: 1973.

166. Reading, Marquess of. *Rufus Isaacs, First Marquess of Reading* by his son. London: Hutchinson, 1942–1945. 2 vols.

See also no. 152.

167. Reynolds, Reginald. *To Live in Mankind: A Quest for Gandhi*. London: Andre Deutsch, 1951. 215.

This is a lively personal account of Reynolds' visit as a young man to Gandhi's Sabarmati Ashram and of his impressions of Gandhi. Reynolds was present when Gandhi was arrested in March 1922. He had earlier been chosen by Gandhi to deliver Gandhi's February 1922 letter to the Viceroy, which was an ultimatum announcing Gandhi's intention to launch mass civil disobedience. Published in the United States as *Quest for Gandhi*. New York: Doubleday, 1952.

168. Rowlatt, Justice. "Report of Committee Appointed to Investigate Revolutionary Conspiracies in India." London: H.M.S.O. Cmnd 9190. 1918.

The report that recommended suspending civil liberties in order to prevent sedition and led to the Rowlatt Act which prompted mass satyagraha.

169. Sitaramayya, B. P. *The History of the Indian National Congress*. Vol. l. (1885–1935). Madras: Working Committee of the Congress, 1935. 1038.

170. Spear, Perceval. *The Oxford History of Modern India 1740–1947*. Oxford: Oxford University Press, 1978. 472. Second Edition.

This standard history covers the unfolding of the national independence movement in Book 4, "National India." The first edition was published in 1965.

171. Swinson, Arthur. *Six Minutes to Sunset: The Story of General Dyer and the Amritsar Affair*. London: Peter Davies, 1964. 216. (See also nos. 149 and 164.)

172. Tendulkar, D. G. *Gandhi in Champaran*. New Delhi: Government of India, 1957. 115.

Account of Gandhi's first major campaign in India, among the indigo planters of Champaran, by his official biographer.

173. Watson, Francis. *The Trial of Mr Gandhi*. London: Macmillan, 1969. 288.

The title refers to Gandhi's trial in March 1922 after the first nationwide civil disobedience campaign, though the book also covers Gandhi's actions up to his death in 1948.

See also: Gene Sharp, *Gandhi Wields the Weapon of Moral Power* (Section VI); Joan Bondurant, *Conquest of Violence*; R. R. Diwakar, *Satyagraha* (Section IX); and the more substantial biographies in Section III.A.

Articles

174. Amin, S. "Gandhi as Mahatma: Gorakhpur District Eastern U.P., 1921–2." In R. Guha, ed., *Subaltern Studies III. Writings on South Asian History and Society*. Delhi: Oxford University Press, 1984.

175. Andrews, C. F. "Day with Mahatma Gandhi." *Atlantic Monthly* 134 (November 1924): 668–71.

176. _____ . "Gandhi as a Religious Teacher." *Living Age* 321 (3 May 1924): 845–51; see also: "Home Rule and Homespun." *Living Age* 320 (8 March 1924): 464–67.

177. _____ . "Leader of the Non-cooperation Movement in India." *International Review of Missions* 13 (April 1924): 190–204.

178. Beaman, F.C.O. "Gandhi: King of India." *New Statesman* 17 (17 September 1921): 639–41.

179. _____ . "Sermon in the Abbey." *Blackwood's Magazine* 215 (June 1924): 869–76.

180. Bond, B. "Amritsar, 1919." *History Today* 13 (October 1963): 666–76. See also "Discussion" 13 (December 1963): 873.

181. Brown, W. N. "Gandhi and the Hungerstrike in India." *South Atlantic Quarterly* 21 (July 1922): 203–9.

182. Buck, P. M., Jr. "Is This the Passing of Mr Gandhi?" *Virginia Quarterly Review* 2 (July 1926): 390–404.

183. Candler, E. "Mahatma Gandhi." *Atlantic Monthly* 130 (July 1922): 105–14.

184. Cape, C. P. "Mohandas Karamchand Gandhi." *London Quarterly Review* 138 (October 1922): 249–52.

185. Case, C. M. "Gandhi and the Indian National Mind." *Journal of Applied Sociology* 7 (July 1923): 293–301.

186. Cooper, V. I. "Gandhi and the Untouchables." *Open Court* 40 (June 1926): 382–84.

187. Das, Tarak Nath. "M. K. Gandhi and the Struggle for Independence in India." *Open Court* 36 (January 1922): 17–21.

188. Das, T. "Progress of the Non-violent Revolution in India." *Journal of International Relations* 12 (October 1921): 204–14.

189. Eddy, S. "Gandhi: An Interpretation." *Christian Century* 40 (19 April 1923): 489–94.

190. Emerson, G. "Gandhi, Religious Politician." *Asia* 22 (May 1922): 389–95.

191. Ewer, W. N. "Close to the Indian Crisis." *Asia* 24 (July 1924): 532–40.

See also the reply by C. Sorabji in issue of September 1924, pp. 716–20.

192. Frank, G. "Who is Gandhi?" *Century* 102 (July 1921): 478–80.

193. "Gandhi and the Crisis in India." *New Republic* 30 (29 March 1922): 124–26.

194. "Gandhi at First Hand." *Atlantic Monthly* 129 (May 1922): 709–11.

195. "Gandhi, Britain's Foe in India." *Current History* the Magazine of the *New York Times* 14 (May 1921): 235–38.

196. "Gandhi, the Great Leader of India." *Review of Reviews* 63 (March 1921): 315–16.

197. Gour, H. S. "Gandhism—and after." *Living Age* 309 (14 May 1921): 389–96.

198. Govil, H. G. "Letter from Gandhi." *Forum* 67 (May 1922): 376–80.

199. Haussding, H. "Bei Mahatma Gandhi im Ashram Sabarmati." *Westermanns Monatschefte* 143 (May 1927): 79–83.

200. Henningham, S. "The Social Setting of the Champaran Satyagraha: The Challenge to an Alien Elite." *The Indian Economic and Social History Review* 13, 1 (January–March 1976): 59–73.

201. Hutchins, G. "Gandhi in the Villages." *World Tomorrow* 10 (May 1927): 202–204.

202. "India: the Political Chaos." *Round Table* 15 (March 1925): 335–52.

203. "Indian Paradox." *Cornhill Magazine* 59 (September 1925): 291–302.

204. Joachim, M. "India Turns Away from Gandhi." *Current History* the Magazine of the *New York Times* 17 (December 1922): 462–71.

205. Jones, E. S. "Soul of Mahatma Gandhi." *World Tomorrow* (December 1924): 367–78.

206. "Latest Thing in Revolutions." *Current Opinion* 72 (April 1922): 445–48.

207. Law, M., and G. Law. "Gandhi in Jail." *Outlook* 130 (19 April 1922): 649–51.

208. Leger, J. A. "Mahatma Gandhi." *Revue de Paris* 29: Part 2 (1 April 1922): 634–43.

209. Londres, A. "Dans l'Inde." *Les Annales Politiques et Litteraires* 81 (26 August 1928): 228–29.

210. Low, D. A. "The Government of India and the First Non-Co-operation Movement—1920–1922." *The Journal of Asian Studies* 25, 2 (1966).

211. Metta, V. B. "Nationalism Marches on in India." *Current History* the Magazine of the *New York Times* 17 (January 1923): 614–17.

212. Mishra, G. "Socio-Economic Background of Gandhi's Champaran Movement." *The Indian Economic and Social History Review* 5 (September 1968): 245–75.

213. Misra, B. "Ides of March in India." *Current History* the Magazine of the *New York Times* 16 (August 1922): 815–20.

214. Mukerji, D. G. "India's Social Revolution." *American Review* 2 (May 1924): 279–82.

215. Mukerji, D. G. "Mahatma Gandhiki jai." *Atlantic Monthly* 133 (June 1924): 721–31.

216. "Non-co-operation and Mr Gandhi." *Round Table* 12 (June 1922): 623–31.

217. O'Dwyer, M. F. "Gandhi and the Prince's Visit to India." *Fortnightly Review* 117 (February 1922): 191–203.

218. O'Dwyer, M. F. "India without Mr Montagu and Gandhi." *Fortnightly Review* 118 (August 1922): 212–29.

219. O'Shashnain, B. P. "Hind-Swaraj." *Catholic World* 115 (July 1922): 487–99.

220. Pearson, W. W. "Gandhi: an Indian Saint." *New Republic* 27 (July 1921): 240–42.

221. Rai, Lajpat. "Gandhi and Non-cooperation." *Nation* 113 (21 December 1921): 722–24.

222. Remzie, T.H.K. "Since Gandhi's Imprisonment." *World Tomorrow* 7 (December 1924): 368–70.

223. Rolland, R. "Mahatma Gandhi." *Century* 107 (December 1923–February 1924): 163–81, 389–405, 590–604.

224. Roy, B. K. "World Will Hear More of Gandhi." *Independent and Weekly Review* 105 (30 April 1921): 443–44.

225. Roy, E. "Gandhi, Revolutionary Mystic." *Living Age* 319 (20 October 1923): 110–15.

226. Roy, E. "Mahatma Gandhi: Revolutionary or Counter-revolutionary?" *Labour Monthly* 5 (September 1923): 158–67.

227. Sexton, B. "Gandhi's Weaponless Revolt in India." *Current History* the Magazine of the *New York Times* 15 (February 1922): 745–52.

228. Sexton, B. "Trial of Gandhi." *Current History* the Magazine of the *New York Times* 16 (June 1922): 440–44.

229. Speer, R. E. "Politics and Missions in India Today." *Missionary Review of the World* 45 (April 1922): 259–64.

230. Ward, H. F. "Gandhi and the Future of India." *Christian Century* 42 (4 June 1925): 727–29.

231. Watson, B. "Passive Resistance or Soul Force." *Open Court* 35 (December 1921): 715–19.

232. Wilson, P. W. "Gandhi as India's Prophet." *Review of Reviews* 65 (May 1922): 449–53.

VI. Gandhi's Role in the Struggle for Indian Independence: 1930–1939

Books

233. Azad, Maulana Abul Kalam. *India Wins Freedom: The Complete Version.* Hyderabad: Orient Longman, 1988. 283.

Azad, a prominent Muslim in the Congress Party (and elected President of Congress in 1939) gives his account of the period 1935–1948. Azad includes detailed references to his own contacts with Gandhi and Gandhi's views and actions. This edition is a revised version of Azad's book published by Sangam Books, London in 1959.

234. Bakshi, S. P. *Gandhi and Dandi March.* New Delhi: Criterion Publications, 1988. 174.

This is an account of the historical background to Gandhi's 1930 Salt March, which launched mass civil disobedience, and of the March itself. It draws heavily on Gandhi's own speeches and writings.

235. Brailsford, H. N. *Rebel India.* New York: New Republic Inc., 1931. 262.

This contemporary record of the 1930–1931 Salt Satyagraha and the non-cooperation movement was written by a British journalist who was a friend of Gandhi.

236. Brown, Judith M. *Gandhi and Civil Disobedience: The Mahatma in Indian Politics, 1928–1934*. Cambridge: Cambridge University Press, 1977. 414.

Brown supplements her earlier study of Gandhi's rise to political influence (see no. 143) with a detailed analysis of Gandhi's role in a key phase of the struggle for independence, drawing upon published and unpublished sources from the standpoint of both the Congress Party and the British government.

237. Churchill, Winston. *The Second World War*. Vol. 1. "The Gathering Storm." London: Cassell, 1948. 724.

Churchill refers briefly (pp. 26–27) to Gandhi's visit to London for the Second Round Table Conference. Churchill also explains why he broke with the Prime Minister, Baldwin, over Gandhi's release from prison and why he believed that the Government's policy would lead to the "loss" of India.

238. Coatman, John. *Years of Destiny: India 1926–1932*. London: Jonathan Cape, 1932. 384. Foreword by Lord Irwin, Viceroy of India, 1926–1931.

239. Coupland, Reginald. *The Indian Problem, 1833–1935*. London: Oxford University Press, 1943, 160. Vol. 1, "Report on the Constitutional Problem in India."

240. Edwardes, Michael. *The Last Years of British India*. London: Cassell, 1963. 205. A study of Indian history from 1914 to 1947 which includes critical analysis of Gandhi's role and of the nonviolent campaigns.

241. Glendevon, J. *The Viceroy at Bay: Lord Linlithgow in India 1936–1943*. London: Collins, 1971. 288.

Includes Linlithgow's assessments of Gandhi.

242. Government of India. *India in 1930–31: A Statement Prepared for Presentation to Parliament*. Calcultta: Government of India Central Publication Branch, 1932. 752.

Chapter 2 and Appendices 2–4 focus on the independence campaign.

243. Irwin, Lord. *Indian Problems: Speeches by Lord Irwin*. London: Allen and Unwin, 1932. 376.

These speeches, made while Lord Irwin (later Lord Halifax) was Viceroy of India (1926–1931) include quite extensive comments on the Salt Satyagraha and mass civil disobedience in 1930–1931. See pp. 74–115, 293–301 and 321–25.

244. Lester, Muriel. *Entertaining Gandhi*. London: Ivor Nicholson and Watson, 1932. 246.

Muriel Lester recounts Gandhi's stay at Kingsley Hall in East London during the Second Round Table Conference and his visits to other sympathisers in England. She also covers his return journey via Paris, Switzerland and Italy to India and to prison.

245. Miller, Webb. *I Found No Peace: The Journal of a Foreign Correspondent*. New York: Simon and Schuster, 1936. 332.

Chapters 16–19 and 21 are relevant to Gandhi and the movement in India.

246. Pyarelal [Nair]. *The Epic Fast*. Ahmedabad: Mohanlal Magnalal Bhatt, 1932. 328.

Gandhi's secretary gives a detailed account of the September 1932 fast which Gandhi undertook while in prison to protest against the British proposal for a separate electorate for the untouchables. The fast roused Hindu conscience about untouchability and resulted in an end to the proposed separate electorate but an increase in the seats to be reserved for untouchables in the legislature.

247. _____. *A Pilgrimage for Peace: Gandhi and Frontier Gandhi among the North West Frontier Pathans*. Ahmedabad: Navajivan, 1950. 216.

Firsthand report on Gandhi's 1938 visit to the North West Frontier and his cooperation with Pathan leader Abdul Gaffar Khan, who led his warlike compatriots in a nonviolent struggle for independence.

248. Sharp, Gene. *Gandhi Wields the Weapon of Moral Power: Three Case Histories.* Ahmedabad: Navajivan, 1960. 316.

Sharp, an expert on nonviolent action, examines three key examples of Gandhi's use of satyagraha: Champaran 1917–1918; the 1930–1931 independence campaign and Gandhi's last fast in January 1948 to quell Muslim-Hindu riots in Delhi. The bulk of the book, however, is an analysis of the nationwide 1930–1931 campaign; see pp. 37–226.

249. Sykes, Sir Frederick. *From Many Angles: An Autobiography.* London: Harrap, 1942. 592.

Sykes was Governor of Bombay in 1928–1933 and so had personal experience of the campaign for independence from the standpoint of the British Raj. Chapters 13–20 cover the period 1928–1942.

See also: M. K. Gandhi, *India's Case for Swaraj* (Section II); James D. Hunt, *Gandhi in London* (Section III.A); S. Gopal, *The Viceroyalty of Lord Irwin*, D. A. Low, *Congress and the Raj* and B. N. Pande, ed., *A Centenary History of the Indian National Congress* (Section V).

Articles

250. Blyth, E.M.E. "Mahatma Gandhi: A Study in Destructiveness." *Quarterly Review* 256 (April 1931): 388–401.

251. Bolton, G. "Mr Gandhi's Vindication; Congress and the Challenge of Democracy." *Great Britain and the East* 49 (15 July 1937): 80.

252. Brailsford, H. N. "Why India Follows Gandhi." *The Forum* 85 (May 1931): 286–92.

253. "Congress at the Crossroads." *Round Table* 29 (September 1939): 775–81.

254. Diettrich, F. "Mahatma Gandhi." *Deutsche Rundschau* 221 (October 1929): 50–55.

255. Fang, Fu-an. "What has Gandhi to offer China?" *China Weekly Review* 52 (30 March 1930): 168–70.

256. Freund, R. "Mahatma Gandhi." *Spectator* 161 (18 November 1938): 854–55.

   See also reply by J. D. Jenkins (30 December 1938): 1125–26.

257. Holland, R. "Mr Gandhi's Arrest: Was it Inevitable?" *Asiatic Review:new series* 28 (April 1932): 250–67.

258. Hossain, S. "Gandhi: Saint and Statesman." *Open Court* 45 (November 1931): 670–75.

259. Houghton, B. "Communal Award and Gandhi." *Labour Monthly* 14 (December 1932): 765–68.

260. "India: Mr Gandhi Again." *Round Table* 23 (September 1933): 807–22.

261. "Indian Problem: The Struggle for the Untouchables." *Review of Reviews* (London) (October 1932): 19–24.

262. Kirk, W. "Will India Follow Gandhi?" *Sociology and Social Research* 14 (March 1930): 342–57.

263. "Mahatma Gandhi's Explanation." *Round Table* 20 (March 1930): 333–34.

264. Matthews, B. "New India: Some Trends and Personalities." *Asiatic Review: new series* 33 (April 1937): 259–61.

265. "Mr Gandhi and the Congress." *Round Table* 24 (December 1933): 131–38.

266. "Mr Gandhi's Fast." *Round Table* (December 1932): 152–59.

267. "Mr Gandhi's Fast." *Round Table* (June 1939): 598–602.

268. Motvani, K. L. "Propaganda in Mahatma Gandhi's Movement." *Social Forces* 8 (June 1930): 574–81.

269. Pernot, M. "L'implacable douceur de Gandhi." *Journal des Debats* (18 April 1930): 619–21; "L'arrestation de Gandhi" (9 May 1930): 733.

270. Petrasch, C. "Interview with Gandhi." *Labour Monthly* 14 (April 1932): 217–24.

271. Rice, S. "Mr Gandhi and the Communal Award." *Asiatic Review: new series* 28 (October 1932): 657–63.

272. Saklatvala, S. "Who is this Gandhi?" *Labour Monthly* 12 (July 1930): 413–17.

273. Sarkar, Sumit. "Logic of Gandhian Nationalism: Civil Disobedience and the Gandhi-Irwin Pact (1930–31)." *The Indian Historical Review* 3, 1 (July 1976).

274. Sarkar, Tanika. "The First Phase of Civil Disobedience in Bengal, 1930–1." *The Indian Historical Review* 4, 1 (July 1977).

VII.   The Second World War and the Quit India Movement: 1939–1945

Books

275. Amery, L. S. *The Empire At Bay: The Amery Diaries, 1929–1945*. Edited by John Barnes and David Nichols. London: Hutchinson, 1988. 1152.

Amery was a Conservative imperialist prominent in British politics and Secretary of State for India in the Second World War cabinet. His diaries include comments on the Cripps Mission and Indian politics during the war.

276. Bhuyan, Arun Chandra. *The Quit India Movement: The Second World War and Indian Nationalism*. New Delhi: Manas, 1975. 262.

Study which draws on recently opened archives of Government of India and includes previously unpublished official correspondence, as well using the Gandhi and Nehru archives. Chapters 2 and 3 cover the Quit India campaign and chapter 5 Gandhi's fast.

277. Chopra, P. N., ed. *Quit India Movement: British Secret Report*. Faridabad, Haryana: Thomson Press (India) Limited, 1976. 407.

This book publishes "Wickenden's Report on the Disturbances of 1942–43," the British India Government's asessment of the movement using intelligence reports, interrogations, intercepted letters and other sources. It appends the secret evidence that was the basis of the report.

278. Churchill, Winston. *The Second World War.* Vol. 3. "The Grand Alliance." London: Cassell, 1950. 716.

This volume of Churchill's monumental account of the Second World War and his role in it includes his January 1942 letter in response to the Cabinet's proposals for a new constitution for India (pp. 614–15). It also includes his letter to the Viceroy about the wholesale release of satyagrahi prisoners, which would be "proclaimed as a victory for Gandhi's party" (p. 748).

279. Churchill, Winston. *The Second World War.* Vol. 4. "The Hinge of Fate." London: Cassell, 1951. 917.

Churchill describes the Japanese threat to India and the creation of a Cabinet Committee to advise the War Cabinet on India. He also notes President Roosevelt's interest in India and proposal for an interim Indian government and the Cripps Mission (pp. 182–96). There are later brief comments on the arrests of Gandhi and Nehru in August 1942 (p. 456) and on Gandhi's three-week fast (pp. 660–61). Churchill concludes that the British government handled the situation correctly.

280. Coupland, Reginald. *Indian Politics, 1936–42.* London: Oxford University Press, 1944. 244. Vol. 2, "Report on the Constitutional Problem in India" (see no. 239).

There is a chapter on the Quit India campaign.

281. Estorick, Eric. *Stafford Cripps a Biography.* London: William Heinemann, 1949. 378. Includes an account of the 1942 Cripps Mission to India.

282. Gilbert, Martin. *Road to Victory: Winston S. Churchill 1941–1945*. Vol. 7 of authorized biography. London: Heinemann, 1417.

Fairly brief but quite illuminating references to Churchill's perception of "Quit India" campaign, Gandhi's imprisonment and fast (pp. 123, 209, 342–43 and 348).

283. Government of India. *Congress Responsibility for Disturbances (1942–43)*. New Delhi: Government of India Press. 1943.

284. Heath, Carl. *Gandhi*. London: Allen and Unwin, 1944. 30.

Pamphlet sympathetically outlining Gandhi's ideas, though includes some criticism of Gandhi's and Congress Party's actions since 1939. Author was member of the Indian Conciliation Group in 1931.

285. Hutchinson, Francis G. *India's Revolution: Gandhi and the Quit India Movement*. Cambridge, Mass.: Harvard University Press, 1973. 326.

The author draws heavily on "interviews with surviving participants and on the secret records of the British government, which have only recently become available" and which revealed how widespread the movement was. This book was first published as: *Spontaneous Revolution: The Quit India Movement*. Delhi: Manohar Book Service, 1971.

286. Mansergh, Nicholas. *Survey of British Commonwealth Affairs, 1939–1952*. Vol. 2. London: Oxford University Press, 1958. (Vol. 1 covered the period 1931–1939.)

287. Menon, V. P. *The Transfer of Power in India*. New Delhi: Orient Longman, 1957. 543.

Book covers the period 1939 to 1947. Menon was Constitutional Adviser to the Governor-General from 1942 to 1947. There are numerous references to Gandhi.

288. Moon, P., ed. *Wavell: The Viceroy's Journal*. London: Oxford University Press, 1973. 528.

Wavell made daily notes during his period as Viceroy from June 1943 to March 1947 and commented quite frequently on Gandhi, whom he described (p. 495) as a "shrewd, malevolent old politician." The editor comments that since Wavell's "very unfavourable judgement" of Gandhi is historically important, the critical comments have not been omitted.

289. Moore, R. J. *Churchill, Cripps and India 1939–1945*. Oxford: Clarendon Press, 1979. 152.

This is a scholarly account of Stafford Cripps's first visit to India, in September to December 1939 and subsequent offers by the British Government to the Indian nationalists; and of Cripps's second mission to India in March and April 1942 and the abortive negotiations up to June 1945.

290. Patil, V. T. *Gandhi, Nehru and the Quit India Movement; A Study in the Dynamics of a Mass Movement*. Delhi: B.R. Publishing Corporation, 1984. 96.

The aim of this study is to examine the roles played by Gandhi and Nehru in the Quit India Movement, drawing on British government documents, in particular the Wickenden Report (see Chopra, no. 277).

291. Pyarelal [Nair]. *Mahatma Gandhi, The Last Phase*. Ahmedabad: Navajivan. 2 vols. 1956 and 1958. 730 and 887.

The two volumes cover Gandhi's role from the Quit India campaign launched in 1942 to his death. Pyarelal was Gandhi's secretary and companion during this period.

See also for this period: M. K. Gandhi, *Gandhiji's Correspondence with the Government: 1942–1944* (Section II); Maulana Azad, *India Wins Freedom* (Section VI).

Articles

292. Fells, H. J. "India: Retrospect and Prospect." *Asiatic Review* 39 (new series) (October 1943): 395–99.

293. French, J. C. "Magic and Politics." *National Review* 120 (April 1943): 298–303.

294. "Gandhi-Jinnah Conversations." *Round Table* 35 (December 1944): 64–67.

295. "Mr Gandhi's Reappearance." *Round Table* 34 (September 1944): 349–53.

296. "Is Gandhi an Insuperable Obstacle?" *Amerasia* 6 (November 1942): 416–18.

297. Shahani, R. G. "Moral Challenge to India: An Open Letter to Mahatma Gandhi." *Asiatic Review* 36 (new series) (January 1940): 155–57.

Printed also in *Spectator* 164 (12 January 1940): 36–37.

See also: "Dangerous Illusions: A Letter to Mr Gandhi." *Spectator* 164 (10 May 1940): 654.

298. Venkataramani, M. S., and B. K. Shrivastava. "President and the Mahatma: America's Response to Gandhi's Fast, February–March 1943." *International Review of Social History* 13, 2 (1966): 141–73.

299. Watson, A. "End to Gandh-ism." *Great Britain and the East* 58 (10 January 1942): 10–11.

See also other articles by Watson in the same journal: "Gandhism the Blight of India." 58 (30 May 1942): 9; "Open Rebellion—Gandhi." 59 (25 July 1942): 10–11; "Passing of Gandhi." 59 (8 August 1942): 12–13; "Folly Supreme in India." 59 (15 August 1942): 11–12; and "Firm Hand in India." 59 (19 September 1942): 13–14.

300. "Why Gandhi and Jinnah Failed: with text of correspondence." *Amerasia* 8 (3 November 1944): 307–19.

301. Wrench, E. "India at the Cross-roads; Interview with Mr. Gandhi." *Spectator* 168 (6 March 1942): 226–27.

VIII.   Independence, Partition and Gandhi's Final Campaigns: 1945–1948

Books

302. Attlee, Clement. *As It Happened.* London: Heinemann, 1954. 227.

Autobiography of the Labour Prime Minister from 1945 to 1951. Attlee discusses the Labour Government's approach to granting Indian independence in the chapter on Commonwealth relations: pp. 179–87.

303. Burridge, Trevor. *Clement Attlee.* London: Jonathan Cape, 1985. 401.

This biography of Attlee covers the granting of independence to India, pp. 268–88.

304. Campbell-Johnson, Alan. *Mission with Mountbatten.* London: Robert Hale, 1951. Reprinted 1972.

305. Collins, Larry, and Dominique Lapierre. *Freedom at Midnight.* London: Grafton Books (Collins), 1982. 596.

Lively detailed account of Mounbatten's role as the last Viceroy of India in 1947 as he tried to find a formula for independence and partition. Written from Mountbatten's point of view and stresses his cordial relations wih Nehru and Gandhi.

306. Fischer, Louis. *A Week with Gandhi*. London: Allen and Unwin, 1943. 122.

Fischer stayed in Gandhi's Sevagram ashram and kept a detailed record of conversations with Gandhi and on his lifestyle.

307. Gandhi, Manubehn. *Last Glimpses of Bapu*. Delhi: Shiva Lal Agarwala and Co., 1962. 348.

Manubehn was Gandhi's great-niece and only constant companion in his last months. This is her diary for January 1948.

308. _____ . *The Lonely Pilgrim: Gandhiji's Noakhali Pilgrimage*. Ahmedabad: Navajivan, 1964. 273.

Record of Gandhi's walk through Noakhali, Bengal, between December 1946 and March 1947 trying to reconcile Muslims and Hindus and end the riots in the region.

309. _____ . *The Miracle of Calcutta*. Ahmedabad: Navajivan, 103.

Account of Gandhi's fast to end the 1947 riots between Hindus and Muslims in the city by his great-niece and companion in that period.

310. Harris, Kenneth. *Attlee*. London: Weidenfeld and Nicolson, 1982. 630.

Biography of the Labour Prime Minister. Chapter 21, "The End of Empire: India," explains briefly the background to Indian independence and outlines the Attlee Government's policy from July 1945 to 1947.

311. Hodson, H. V. *The Great Divide: Britain—India—Pakistan*. London: Hutchinson, 1969. 563.

The author of this book was Constitutional Adviser to the Viceroy from 1941 to 1942 and has drawn on Mountbatten's India archive and Stafford Cripps's papers. He examines both the growing rift between Britain and the Indian Empire and the growing rift between Hindus and Muslims that led to Partition. Includes an assessment of Gandhi's personality (pp. 33–36) and includes frequent references to Gandhi's policies and role in events.

312. Moore, R. J. *Escape from Empire: The Atlee Government and the Indian Problem.* Oxford: Oxford University Press, 1983. 376.

Examination of how Britain granted independence to India and Pakistan, which traces the evolution of Labour Party policies and the specific contribution made by Attlee and Cripps. It aims to redress the bias of earlier acounts from the perspective of those serving in India or working with Mountbatten.

313. Mosley, Leonard. *The Last Days of the British Raj.* London: Weidenfeld and Nicolson, 1961. 263.

Book that sets out to examine British policy on partition and the date for independence and in particular how far Wavell tried to promote agreement between Congress and the Muslim League and why Attlee decided to expedite British withdrawal. Includes accounts of Gandhi's role in the negotiations and his attempts to stop the communal riots.

314. Sankhdher, M. M. l982. *Gandhi, Gandhism, and the Partition of India.* New Delhi: Deep and Deep Publications, 1982.

315. Sharp, Gene. *Gandhi Faces the Storm.* Ahmedabad: Navajivan, 1961. 71.

Explores Gandhi's inner struggles from 1946 to his death in January 1948 to understand the tragedies of partition and the Hindu-Muslim riots.

316. Sheean, Vincent. *Lead Kindly Light.* London: Cassell, 1950. 397.

The title is taken from Gandhi's favourite hymn. Sheean travelled to India in 1945. He summarizes Gandhi's life (pp. 67–172), but the main emphasis of the book is on religious issues. He discusses the Gita and Gandhi's interpretation of it and his own religious conversion. Sheean met Gandhi in January 1948 and attended his prayer meetings.

317. Tuker, Lieutenant General Sir Francis. *While Memory Serves*. London: Vassett, 1950.

Tuker's autobiography covers his service in India in the run-up to Independence and includes his memories of the Hindu-Muslim riots in Calcutta in August 1947 when he was in command there.

318. Ziegler, Philip. *Mountbatten: The Official Biography*. London: Collins, 1985. 786.

Chapters 28–38 cover Mountbatten's period in India from 1947 to 1948 as the last Viceroy, with a remit to transfer independence to the subcontinent as soon as possible, and as the first Governor-General in independent India. Ziegler covers the whole process of transferring power, but includes fairly frequent references to Gandhi's activities and summarizes Mountbatten's interviews with him.

See also: M. K. Gandhi, *Gandhiji's Correspondence with the Government: 1944–1947* (Section II); N. Mansergh and Penderel Moon, eds., *The Transfer of Power*, vols. 9–12 (Section I); G. Catlin, *In the Path of Mahatma Gandhi*, which includes a section on the author's journeying in India in 1947; B. Chandiwala, *At the Feet of Bapu*, which lays special emphasis on the later period and W. L. Shirer, *Gandhi. A Memoir* (Section III.A); N. K. Bose, *My Days with Gandhi*, which describes Gandhi's struggles against communal bloodshed in 1946 to 1947 (Section III.B); Sharp, Gene, *Gandhi Wields the Weapon of Moral Power* (Section VI), which includes an account of Gandhi's last fast, to quell Hindu-Muslim riots in Delhi in 1948 and V.P. Menon, *The Transfer of Power* (Section VII).

Articles

319. Alexander, H. "Gandhi and the Cabinet Mission in 1946." *Contemporary Review* 190 (September 1956): 172–76.

   Review of P. Nayyar, *Mahatma Gandhi: The Last Phase.*

320. "Assassination of Mahatma Gandhi." *Round Table* 38 (March 1948): 588–92.

321. Dutt, R. P. "Gandhi—the Last Phase." *Labour Monthly* 30 (March 1948): 30.

322. Eidlitz, W. "Mahatma Gandhi: zum jahrestag der unabhaengigkeitserklaerung Indiens." *Deutsche Rundschau* 76 (January/February 1950): 25–31.

323A. Preece, R. B. "Gandhi." *Hibbert Journal* 44 (July 1946): 305–11.

For assessments of Gandhi at the time of his assassination see Section X.

IX. Gandhi's Social, Political and Ethical Thought and Practice

This section does not attempt to include everything written about Gandhi's social or political philosophy, or his moral and religious teachings. It is also selective about the now-extensive literature on the theory and practice of nonviolent action. The aim here is to indicate the range of sympathetic and critical analyses available on all facets of Gandhi's thought and on nonviolent approaches influenced by him. A few of the most widely recommended books have been starred.

Books

323B. Agarwal, Shriman Narayan. *Relevance of Gandhian Economics*. Ahmedabad: Navajivan, 1970. 256.

Discusses the Gandhian concept of sarovdaya and compares with the Marxist approach to social and economic development.

324. Andrews, Charles F. *Mahatma Gandhi's Ideas, Including Selections from His Writings*. London: Allen and Unwin, 1929. 382.

325. Bandyopahyaya, Jayantanuja. *Social and Political Thought of Gandhi*. Bombay and New York: Allied Publishers, 1969. 414.

Critical examination by a social scientist of Gandhi's thought in relation to contemporary national and international developments.

326. *Bondurant, Joan V. *Conquest of Violence: The Gandhian Philosophy of Conflict.* London: Oxford University Press, 1958. 269.

Examines concept and practice of satyagraha in relation both to Hinduism and Western political thought. Includes detailed analysis of three of Gandhi's campaigns in India: the 1918 Ahmedabad textile workers' dispute, the 1919 nationwide resistance to the Rowlatt Bills, and the 1930–1931 Salt March and civil disobedience. Examines also the Vykom Temple Road and Bardoli campaigns conducted on Gandhian lines but not under Gandhi's direct leadership.

327. Borman, William. *Gandhi and Non-Violence.* Albany, New York: State University of New York Press, 1986. 287.

Critical study of Gandhi's philosophy of nonviolence, examining its metaphysics, ideology, practical applications and limits. Borman comments on Gandhi's apparently inconsistent stance on war.

328. Bose, Nirmal K. *Studies in Gandhism.* Calcutta: Indian Associated Publishing Co., 1947. 359.

Collection of essays, including one critical of nonviolence, edited by a co-worker with Gandhi. This is a substantially revised version of the original edition published in 1940.

329. Bose, R. N. *Gandhian Technique and Tradition in Industrial Relations.* Calcutta: All India Institute of Social Welfare and Business Management, 1956. 228.

330. Brock, Peter. *The Mahatma and Mother India.* Ahmedabad: Navajivan, 1983. 223.

Selection of essays on both nonviolence and Gandhi's nationalism. The explorations of nationalism include "The Emergence of

Gandhi's Cultural Nationalism," "Populism and the Shaping of Gandhi's National Idea" and "Gandhi's Idea of Hindustani." Useful references and footnotes.

331. *Chatterjee, Margaret. *Gandhi's Religious Thought*. London: Macmillan, 1983. 194.

Analysis of Gandhi's religious ideas in relation to Indian traditions and Christianity and the integration between Gandhi's religious beliefs and his social and political action. The author was Professor of Philosophy at the University of Delhi.

332. Dasgupta, S. 1984. *Philosophical Assumptions for Training in Non-Violence*. Ahmedabad: Gujarat Vidyapith.

333. Datta, D. M. 1968. *The Philosophy of Mahatma Gandhi*. Calcutta: University of Calcutta. 171.

Originally published in the United States, Madison, Wisconsin: University of Wisconsin Press, 1953.

334. *Dhawan, Gopinath N. 1957. *The Political Philosophy of Mahatma Gandhi*. Ahmedabad: Navajivan, 1957. 3rd edition, 363.

Discusses the metaphysical and ethical bases of Gandhi's approach, the role of leadership in satyagraha and the nature of satyagraha as a means of corporate action and as a way of life. The final chapter examines how Gandhi's concept of a "nonviolent state" might be organized.

335. Diwakar, Ranganath R. *Satyagraha: The Power of Truth*. Hinsdale, Illinois: Regnery, 1948. 108.

This is a brief introductory account. A revised and extended edition was published jointly in 1969 by the Gandhi Peace Foundation, Delhi and Bharatiya Vidya Bhavan, Bombay as *Saga of Satyagraha*. 248 pp.

336. *Gregg, Richard B. *The Power of Nonviolence*. London: James Clark, 1960. 192.

Classic text on nonviolent action, first published 1934, drawing on a range of examples, but particularly inspired by Gandhi and giving particular emphasis to his campaigns and interpretation of nonviolence.

337. Gregg, Richard B. *Which Way Lies Hope: An Examination of Capitalism, Communism, Socialism and Gandhiji's Programme.* Ahmedabad: Navajivan, 1957. 219.

338. Horsburgh, H.J.N. *Non-violence and Aggression: A Study of Gandhi's Moral Equivalent of War.* London: Oxford University Press, 1968. 207.

Examines the bases and practice of Gandhian satyagraha and its possible application to a policy of nonviolent defence in the nuclear age.

339. Hoyland, J. S. *The Cross Moves East: A Study in the Significance of Gandhi's Satyagraha.* London: George Allen and Unwin, 1931. 160.

340. *Iyer, Raghavan N. *The Moral and Political Thought of Mahatma Gandhi.* New York: Oxford University Press, 1973. 449.

Scholarly analysis of Gandhi's ideas, which discusses his views on morality and politics, the perfectability of human nature and individual conscience and heroism. Iyer also analyses the concepts of satya, ahimsa, satyagraha, swaraj and swadeshi, which are central to Gandhi's thought. He draws extensively on Gandhi's own writings.

341. Juergensmeyer, Mark. *Fighting with Gandhi.* New York: Harper and Row, 1984. 182.

Examines Gandhi's theory of social conflict.

342. Kripalani, J. B. *Gandhian Thought.* Bombay: Orient Longmans, 1961. 281.

A compilation of essays, including some written during debates in the 1930s over Marxism and Gandhianism, by an exponent of Gandhi's ideas.

343. _____ . *The Latest Fad: Basic Education*. Sevagram: Hindustania Talimi Sangh, 1948. 94.

An outline of Gandhi's educational scheme for India.

344. Kumarappa, J. C. *The Economy of Permanence:A Quest for a Social Order Based on Nonviolence*. Varanasa: Sarva Seva Sangh, 1958. 208. Earlier published in two parts, 1946 and 1948.

345. Lohia, Rammanohar. *Marx, Gandhi and Socialism*. Hyderabad: Nava Hind Publications, 1963. 550.

Examines how Gandhi's thought could enrich the socialist tradition.

346. Malik, Saroj. *Gandhian Satyagraha and Contemporary World*. Rohtak: Manthan Publications, 1985. 227.

Revised doctoral thesis that examines satyagraha as a technique, satyagraha and the American Civil Rights Movement, satyagraha and war, and Jayaprakash Narayan's concept of "Total Revolution."

347. Mashruwala, K. G. *Gandhi and Marx*. Ahmedabad: Navajivan, 1951. 112.

348. Muzumdar, Ammu Menon. *Social Welfare in India: Mahatma Gandhi's Contributions*. London: Asia Publishing House, 1964. 179.

Covers Gandhi's programmes to promote the welfare of women and untouchables and also rural welfare.

349. Naess, Arne. *Gandhi and Group Conflict: An Exploration of Satyagraha*. Oslo: Universitetsforlanget, 1974. 167.

Norwegian social scientist's analysis of Gandhi's philosophy of conflict. Covers the metaphysics of satyagraha and the norms and hypotheses of Gandhian ethics and strategy of struggle. Compares Gandhi with Luther, Nietzsche, Tolstoy and Jaspars and reflects on nonviolence in relation to contemporary advocacy of revolutionary violence.

350. Naess, Arne. *Gandhi and the Nuclear Age*. Totowa, New Jersey: Bedminister Press, 1965. 149.

Examines Gandhi's political morality in relation to Luther, Hobbes, Nietzsche and Tolstoy, his approach to social conflict and the relevance of Gandhian nonviolence to international politics.

351. Nanda, B. R. *Gandhi: Pan-Islamism, Imperialism and Nationalism*. Delhi: Oxford University Press, 1990. 446.

352. Panter-Brick, Simone. *Gandhi Against Machiavellism: Nonviolence in Politics*. Bombay: Asian Publishing Co., 1966. 240.

353. *Parekh, Bhiku. *Gandhi's Political Philosophy: A Critical Examination*. Notre Dame, Indiana: University of Notre Dame Press, 1989. 248.

Parekh describes Gandhi as "one of the first non-Western thinkers of the modern age to develop a political theory grounded in the unique experience and articulated in terms of the indigenous philosophical vocabulary of his country." Examines Gandhi's critique of modern civilization, his philosophy and religion, political theory and concept of satyagraha. Parekh concludes with a "critical appreciation" of Gandhi's ideas and discusses why he has had so little influence on India since his death.

354. Patil, V. T, ed. *New Dimensions and Perspectives in Gandhism*. New Delhi: Inter-India Publications, 1989. 536.

Compilation of essays by both Indian and Western specialists on Gandhi examining his ideas on a wide range of issues including nationalism, politics, economics, religion, women and the untouchables.

355. Power, Paul F. *Gandhi on World Affairs*. London: Allen and Unwin, 1961. 166.

Critical survey of Gandhi's views on such topics as war, Communism and Indian foreign policy.

356. Power, Paul F., ed. *The Meanings of Gandhi*. Honolulu: University Press of Hawaii, 1971. 199.

357. Ramana Murti, V. V. *Nonviolence in Politics: A Study of Gandhian Techniques and Thinking*. Delhi: Frank Bros and Co., 1958. 246.

Analysis of the nonviolent campaigns in India.

358. Rao, M. B., ed. *Mahatma: A Marxist Symposium*. Bombay: People's Publishing Houses, 1969. 136.

Based on Communist Party of India symposium on Gandhi.

359. Rattan, Rom. *Gandhi's Concept of Political Obligation*. Calcutta: Minerva Associates, 1972. 346.

360. Ray, Sibnarayan, ed. *Gandhi, India and the World: An International Symposium*. Bombay: Nachiketa Publications, 1970. 384; and Melbourne: The Hawthorne Press, 1970.

Includes essays on Gandhi's religious thought, his theory of nonviolence and his political thought. There are also contributions on Gandhi's relations with other important Indian figures—Gokhale, Tagore, Nehru and the Marxist M. N. Roy—exploring both personal links and contrasting ideologies.

361. Richards, Glyn. *The Philosophy of Gandhi: A Study of his Basic Ideas*. Curzon Press and Barnes and Noble, 1982. 178.

Systematic study of Gandhi's philosophy with particular reference to his concept of truth. Discusses the relation of Gandhi's ideas to Hinduism and contemporary philosophers.

362. Sharp, Gene. *Gandhi as a Political Strategist: with Essays on Ethics and Politics*. Boston: Porter Sargent, 1979. 355.

Collection of essays written by leading theorist of nonviolent action and Gandhi scholar between 1959 and 1970. Includes extended review essays of Erik Erikson, *Gandhi's Truth,* and Joan Bondurant, *Conquest of Violence*, plus assessments of Gandhi's relevance to defence policy and elucidation of aspects of his thought. There is an extended bibliography and suggestions for teaching Gandhi.

363. *Sharp, Gene. *The Politics of Nonviolent Action.* 2 vols: "Power and Struggle" and "The Methods of Nonviolent Action." Boston: Porter Sergent, 1973. 902 (both vols.).

Major study of both theory and practice of nonviolent action classifying range of methods and analysing dynamics of nonviolent struggle. The study draws on a very wide range of examples. Gandhi's campaigns are specifically covered in pp. 41–42, 82–87, 211–12 and 277–78.

364. Shridharani, Krishnalal. *War Without Violence: A Study of Gandhi's Method and its Accomplishments.* London: Gollancz, 1939. 288. Reprinted by New York: Garland, 1972. 351.

Explains theory and practice of satyagraha and includes some final comments on the role of nonviolent action in democratic states or in opposing an invasion.

365. Spratt, Philip. *Gandhism: An Analysis.* Madras: Huxley Press, 1939. 516.

Part 1 discusses the man as ascetic, politician and saint; part 2 covers the Khalifat and Rowlatt campaigns and discusses forms of swaraj.

366. Verma, M. M. *Gandhi's Technique of Mass Mobilization.* New Delhi: R. K. Gupta, 1990. 252.

367. Weber, Thomas. *Conflict Resolution and Gandhian Ethics.* New Delhi: Gandhi Peace Foundation, 1991. 180.

See also: Muriel Lester, *Gandhi: World Citizen*, Part l, and George Woodcock, *Gandhi* (Section III.A); S. Radhoakrishnan, ed. *Mahatma Gandhi* (Section X) which includes theoretical assessments by prominent theorists.

Articles

368. Appadorai, A. "Gandhi's Contribution to Social Theory." *Review of Politics* 31 (July 1969): 312–28.

369. Bose, A. "Gandhian Perspectives on Peace." *Journal of Peace Research* 18, 2 (1981): 159–64. Includes a bibliography.

370. Buber, Martin. "Letter to Mahatma Gandhi." In Peter Mayer, ed. *The Pacifist Conscience*. Harmondsworth, Middlesex: Penguin, 1966: 269–82.

Written from Palestine in February 1939 in response to Gandhi's 26 November 1938 article in *Harijan* urging German Jews to use nonviolent (not violent) resistance against Nazism. See also B. B. Kling, "Gandhi, Nonviolence and the Holocaust." *Peace and Change* 16 (April 1991): 176–96.

371. Cenknar, W. "Gandhi and Creative Conflict." *Thought* 45 (Autumn 1970): 421–32.

372. Cornelius, J. J. "Militarism and India's Vision of Christ's Method for World Peace." *Methodist Review* (New York) 108 (November 1925): 890–903.

373. Das, T. "Gandhi and Indian Industrialism." *World Tomorrow* 7 (December 1924) 370–72.

374. De Crespigny, Anthony. "The Nature and Methods of Nonviolent Coercion." *Political Studies* 12 (June 1964): 256–65.

375. De Ligt, B. "Mahatma Gandhi on War: An Open Letter to Gandhi and his Reply." *World Tomorrow* 11 (November 1928): 445–47.

376. Diwan, R. "Economics of Love: or An Attempt at Gandhian Economics." *Journal of Economic Issues* 16 (June 1982): 413–33.

This is one contribution to a Symposium on Gandhian Economics in this issue.

Other articles by W. M. Dugger, D. Kanel and G. Rosen consider Gandhian economics from the perspectives of Ayres, John R. Commons and Schumpeter.

377. Dombrowski, D. A. "Gandhi, Sainthood and Nuclear Weapons." *Philosophy East and West* 33 (October 1983): 401–6.

378. Dube, Ram-Prasad-Duhe. "Social Aspects of Gandhism." *Living Age* 313 (22 April 1922): 209–13.

379. Farber, J. "Violence and Material Class Interests: Fanon and Gandhi." *Journal of Asian and African Studies* 16 (July–October 1981): 196–211.

380. Gupta, S. S. "Gandhi on Labor-Capital, Relations." *American Journal of Economics and Sociology* 30 (October 1971): 429–37.

381. Hendrick, G. "Influence of Thoreau's Civil Disobedience on Gandhi's Satyagraha." *New England Quarterly* 29 (December 1956): 462–71.

382. Hettne, B. "Vitality of Gandhian Tradition." *Journal of Peace Research* 13 (1976): 227–45.

383. Koshal, M. and R. K. "Gandhi's Influence on Indian Economic Planning: A Critical Analysis." *American Journal of Economics and Sociology* 32 (July 1973): 311–30.

384. Kuntz, P. G. "Gandhi's Truth." *International Philosophical Quarterly* 22 (September 1982): 141–55.

385. Lavrin, J. "Tolstoy and Gandhi." *The Russian Review* 19 (April 1960).

386. "Mahatma Gandhi and Tolstoy." *Near East* 36 (28 November 1929): 593–94.

387. Mazrui, A. "Gandhi, Marx and the Warrior Tradition: Towards Androgynous Liberation." *Journal of Asian and African Studies* 12 (January–October 1977): 179–96.

388. Morris-Jones, W. H. "Mahatma Gandhi—Political Philosopher?" *Political Studies* 8 (February 1960): 16–36.

Examines whether there is a "philosophy of politics" to be found in Gandhi's statements.

389. Muzumdar, H. T. "Implications of the Gandhi Technique of Non-Violence for India and the World." *Institute of World Affairs Proceedings* 17 (1939): 209–15.

390. Naess, Arne. "A Systematization of Gandhian Ethics of Conflict Resolution." *Journal of Conflict Resolution* (June 1958).

391. Pantham, T. "Thinking with Mahatma Gandhi: Beyond Liberal Democracy." *Political Theory* 11 (May 1983): 165–80.

392. Parel, A. "Symbolism in Gandhian Politics." *Canadian Journal of Political Science* 2 (December 1969): 513–27.

393. Power, P. F. "Toward a Re-evaluation of Gandhi's Political Thought." *Western Political Quarterly* 16 (March 1963): 99–108.

394. Ramana Murti, V. V. "Buber's Dialogue and Gandhi's Satyagraha." *Journal of the History of Ideas* 29 (October 1968): 605–13.

395. Ramana Murti, V. V. "Satyagraha as an Indo-British Dialogue." *Journal of World History* 10, 4 (1968): 872–90.

396. Richards, G. "Gandhi's Concept of Truth and the Advaita Tradition." *Religious Studies* 22 (March 1986): 1–14.

397. Rivett, K. "Economic Thought of Mahatma Gandhi." *British Journal of Sociology* 10 (March 1959): 1–15. (Bibliography pp. 13–15.)

398. Rolnick, P. J. "Charity, Trusteeship and Social Change in India. A Study of Political Ideology." *World Politics* 14 (April 1962): 493–60.

399. Rothermund, I. "Individual and Society in Gandhi's Political Thought." *Journal of Asian Studies* 28 (February 1969): 313–20.

400. Rudolph, Susanne Hoeber. "The New Courage: An Essay on Gandhi's Psychology." *World Politics* 16 (October 1963): 98–117.

401. Rudolph, Susanne Hoeber. "Self Control and Political Potency: Gandhi's Asceticism." *American Scholar* 35 (Winter 1965–1966): 79–95.

402. Saxena, S. K. "Fabric of Self-Suffering: A Study in Gandhi." *Religious Studies* 12 (June 1976): 239–47.

403. Sorensen, G. "Utopianism in Peace Research: The Gandhian Heritage." *Journal of Peace Research* 29 (May 1992): 135–44.

404. Spodek, H. "On the Origins of Gandhi's Political Methodology: The Heritage of Kathiawad and Gujarat." *Journal of Asian Studies* 30 (February 1971): 361–72.

405. Swarup, S. "Ambivalence of Non-violence." *Political Quarterly* 41 (April 1970): 207–15.

406. Thakur, S. C. "Gandhi's God." *International Philosophical Quarterly* 11 (December 1971): 485–95.

407. Tinker, J. M. "Political Power and Non-violent Resistance: The Gandhian Technique." *Western Political Quarterly* 24 (December 1971): 775–88.

408. Watson, Francis. "Gandhi as a Hunger-Striker?" *Encounter* 57 (November 1981): 62–64.

X. Gandhi's Place in History

Books

409. Bandyopadhyaya, Jayantanuja. *Mao Tse-tung and Gandhi: Perspectives on Social Transformation*. Bombay: Allied, 1973. 156.

Covers historical contexts of Gandhi and Mao and their theories of struggle (Satyagraha and People's War) and of political change. Compares the achievements of each.

410. Copley, Antony. *Gandhi: Against The Tide*. Oxford: Basil Blackwell, 1987. 118.

Brief but informative examination of Gandhi's life, thought and influence, and of historiographic debates, in Historical Association Studies series.

411. Edwardes, Michael. *The Myth of the Mahatma: Gandhi, the British and the Raj*. London: Constable, 1986. 270.

The first three parts of the book cover the making of the Raj, making Sahibs and making nationalism. Only Part Four (pp. 179–260) is on "Making the Mahatma." The author explains the book as a response to the Attenborough film *Gandhi* and the British TV series *The Jewel in the Crown*. Its aim is to put the record straight about the Raj and to combat the myth of Gandhi and the Western tendency to admire his ideas. Edwardes accuses Gandhi of cruelty to his family, sanctifying poverty and the status of the untouchables (harijans) and failing to raise the position of the poor. Gandhi was "essentially anti-modern" and encouraged the "deadweight of Hindu atavism." He notes other critical accounts of Gandhi by Arthur Koestler and Ved Mehta and V. S. Naipaul, *India a Wounded Civilization*, which comments on tradition and the Hindu view of society.

412. Fischer, Louis. *Gandhi and Stalin*. New York: New American Library, 1954. 192.

413. Green, Martin. *The Challenge of the Mahatmas*. New York: Basic Books, 1978. 256.

Based on a series of talks given at Tufts University. On Gandhi and Tolstoy.

Green has also written as a sequel a biographical comparison of Tolstoy and Gandhi, using aesthetic concepts to interpret Gandhi and political concepts to interpret Tolstoy: *Tolstoy and Gandhi, Men of Peace*. New York: Basic Books, 1983. 319.

414. Hick, John, and Lamont C. Hempel, eds. *Gandhi's Significance for Today*. Basingstoke: Macmillan, 1989. 275.

Essays by Gandhi scholars arranged in three sections: Gandhi the Man, Gandhi on Religion and Ethics, and Gandhian Politics and Economics.

415. Gupta, Manmathnath. *Gandhi and His Times*. New Delhi: Lipi Prakashan, 1982. 310.

A very critical assesment of Gandhi's role in the struggle for independence and in the process leading up to partition, as well as of Gandhi's central ideas.

416. Holmes, W.H.G. *The Twofold Gandhi: Hindu Monk and Revolutionary Politician*. London: A. R. Mowbray, 1952. 144.

Written by a Christian missionary in Calcutta who had some contact with Gandhi. Not a biography, but an examination of Gandhi as a champion of the oppressed, his religion, the role of fasting and satyagraha. The author concludes that Gandhi "remains an enigma," a seeker after truth who, as a politican, "packed his statements with untruth."

417. Jones, Marc Edmund. *Gandhi Lives*. Philadelphia: David McKay, 1948. 184.

An assessment of Gandhi after his death commenting on "Gandhi the Statesman" and "the Avatar." Jones also discusses satyagraha, Gandhi's social views and his approach to the Bhagavad-Gita.

418. Jones, E. Stanley. *Mahatma Gandhi: An Interpretation*. London: Hodder and Stoughton, 1948. 208. Reprinted 1983.

Examines Gandhi's death and its meaning and assesses Gandhi's leading ideas and practices and their future relevance.

419. Kapur, S. *Raising Up A Prophet: The African-American Encounter with Gandhi*. Boston, Mass.: Beacon Press, 1992. 222.

Examines influence of Gandhi on the U.S. Civil Rights movement from the 1920s to the 1950s, demonstrating that Martin Luther King was by no means the only leader influenced by Gandhi's campaigns in South Africa and India.

420. Koestler, Arthur. *The Lotus and the Robot*. London: Hutchinson, 1966. 296.

This examination of Asian culture includes an analysis of Gandhi's personality and of his thought. The original 1960 edition was banned in India in 1962 on the grounds that it made objectionable remarks about Gandhi. Koestler sees Gandhi as a Hindu obscurantist.

421. Lewis, Martin Dempsey. *Gandhi: Maker of Modern India.* Lexington, Mass.: D. C. Heath, 1965. 113.

Collection of essays reflecting very diverse political and philosophical views on the importance of Gandhi's life and thought.

422. Mehta, Ved. *Mahatma Gandhi and his Apostles.* London: Andre Deutsch, 1977. 260.

The author uses recordings, memoirs, press clippings and Gandhi's own speeches and writings to try to "demythologize Gandhi and to capture something of the nature of his influence on his followers." He discusses memorials to Gandhi, including the Gandhi National Memorial Fund and Gandhi Peace Foundation. A chapter on Gandhi's family draws on interviews with Gandhi's relations. Part 2 covers Gandhi's life and Part 3 "Nonviolence: Bramacharya and Goat's Milk." Lively, penetrating and deliberately irreverent, but quite sympathetic to Gandhi, if not to all aspects of the Gandhi cult.

423. Moore, Barrington, Jr. *The Social Origins of Dictatorship and Democracy: Lord and Peasant in the Making of the Modern World.* London: Allen Lane, The Penguin Press, 1967. 559.

Chapter 6, "Democracy in Asia: India and the Price of Peaceful Change," includes critical comments on Gandhi. Moore sees Gandhi as seeking a return to an "idealized past" based on the village community, and as the representative of Indian peasants and village artisans (pp. 370–78).

424. Moraes, Frank. *Report on Mao's China.* New York: Macmillan, 1953. 212.

Report on tour of China in 1952 on a Government of India cultural delegation. Includes comparisons betwen Mao and Gandhi.

425. Morris-Jones, W. H. *The Government and Politics of India.* London: Hutchinson, 1971. 280. Third revised edition.

Includes material on "the saintly idiom" in Indian politics which is relevant to Gandhi.

426. Mukerjee, Hiren. *Gandhiji: A Study*. New Delhi: People's Publishing House, 1960. 225. Second revised edition.

Assessment by an Indian Communist of Gandhi's political role.

427. Nanda, B. R. *Gandhi and his Critics*. Delhi: Oxford University Press, 1985.

Looks at controversial isssues in Gandhi's life and thought.

428. Nehru, Jawaharlal. *Nehru on Gandhi: A Selection arranged in the order of events from the writings and speeches of Jawaharlal Nehru*. New York: John Day, 1948. 150.

429. Prasad, Bimla, ed. *Gandhi, Nehru and J. P.: Studies in Leadership*. Delhi: Chanakya, 1985.

Essays by Indian, American and British protagonists and analysts of nonviolence and nonviolent action, for example, Diwakar, Iyer, Bondurant, Muste, Sharp and Alexander. This is a revised and enlarged edition of the book published by the Gandhi Peace Foundation in 1967.

430. Radhakrishnan, S., ed. *Mahatma Gandhi: Essays and Reflections on His Life and Work*. Bombay: Jaico Publishing House, 1956.

Includes a large number of essays on Gandhi by well-known international figures and a memorial section with tributes and extracts from Gandhi's own writings (pp. 359–426). Earlier editions were published by Allen and Unwin in 1939 and 1949.

431. Ramachandran, G., and T. K. Mahadevan, eds. *Gandhi: His Relevance for Our Time*. Berkeley: World Without War Council, 1971. 393.

432. Rudolph, L. I. and S. H. *The Modernity of Tradition: Political Development in India*. Chicago: University of Chicago Press, 1967.

Part 2 covers "The Traditional Roots of Charisma: Gandhi."

Articles

433. Chaudhary, A., and O. R. Bryan. "Mahatma Gandhi: Journalist and Freedom Propagandist." *Journalism Quarterly* 51 (Summer 1974): 286–91.

434. Clymer, K. J. "Samuel Evans Stokes, Mahatma Gandhi and Indian Nationalism." *Pacific Historical Review* 59 (February 1990): 51–76.

435. Davies, D. "Gandhi's Legacy—and the Unlearned Lessons." *Far Eastern Economic Review* 120 (12 May 1983): 36–41.

See also in same issue article by S. Ali, "Gandhian Idealism is Praised not Practised," pp. 41–42.

436. Easwaran, E. "Gandhi—Reflections After the Film." *Cross Currents* 32 (Winter 1982–1983).

437. Fischer, L. "The New Politics of Gandhi: Film Review." *Social Policy* 13 (Spring 1983): 61–64.

438. Francis, R. A. "Romain Rolland and Gandhi: A Study in Communication." *Journal of European Studies* 5 (December 1975): 291–307.

439. Gokhale, B. G. "Gandhi and the British Empire." *History Today* 19 (November 1969): 744–51.

440. Gokhale, B. G. "Gandhi and History." *History and Theory* 11, 2 (1972): 214–25.

441. Goldbloom, M. J. "Death of a Man." *Commentary* (March 1948): 254–55.

442. Grenier, R. "Movies: the Gandhi Nobody Knows." *Commentary* 75 (March 1983): 59–72.

443. Juergensmeyer, M. "The Gandhi Revival—A Review Article." *Journal of Asian Studies* 43 (February 1984): 293–98.

444. Kaye, L. "Glimpses of Gandhi as the Mahatma-in-the-Making." *Far Eastern Economic Review* 142 (20 October 1988): 48–51.

445. Leigh, M. "Martyred Mahatma." *Church Quarterly Review* 146 (April 1948): 1–14.

446. Mandelbaum, D. G. "Study of Life History: Gandhi." *Current Anthropology* 14 (June 1973): 177–206. Includes bibliography.

447. Masani, Zareer. "India's Middle-Class Messiah." *New Statesman* 108 (10 December 1982): 8–9. Comment related to the Attenborough film.

448. Orwell, George. "Reflections on Gandhi." *Partisan Review* 16 (January 1949): 85–92. Reprinted in Orwell, George. *Shooting an Elephant and Other Essays*. New York: Harcourt Brace, 1950. 200.

This is a frequently cited critical assessment of Gandhi.

449. Radhakrishnan, S. "Mahatma Gandhi." *Hibbert Journal* 46 (April 1948): 193–97.

450. Ray, H. "Changing Soviet Views on Mahatma Gandhi." *Journal of Asian Studies* 29 (November 1969): 85–106.

451. Rosenfeld, I. "Gandhi: Self-realization through Politics; the Mystery of Leadership." *Commentary* 10 (August 1950): 131–41.

452. Rumbold, A. "Film, Fact and History." *Encounter* 60 (March 1983): 63–65.

453. Russell, Bertrand. "Mahatma Gandhi." *Atlantic Monthly* 190 (December 1952): 35–39.

454. Smith, T. V. "Saints: Secular and Sacerdotal—James Madison and Mahatma Gandhi." *Ethics* 59 (October 1948): 58–60.

455. Struddert, G. "Gandhi and the Christian Imperialists." *History Today* 40 (October 1990): 19–22.

456. Waghorne, J. P. "Case of the Missing Autobiography." *American Academy of Religion Journal* 49 (December 1981): 589–603.

457. Watson, Francis. "Getting Gandhi Straight." *Encounter* 61 (November 1983): 80.

458. Wyatt, W. "Saint in Politics." *New Statesman and Nation* (7 Februry 1948): 107–8.

459. Younger, S. O. "Gandhi: The Person and the Film." *Theology Today* 40 (July 1983): 168–73.

See also article by P. Younger, "Gandhi: Moral Man in Immoral Society," pp. 174–76.

XI. The Gandhian Movement after Gandhi

Books

460. Del Vasto, Lanza. *Gandhi to Vinoba: The New Pilgrimage.* London: Rider, 1956. 231.

461. _____ . *Return to the Source.* London: Rider, 1971.

Chapter 4 describes Del Vasto's visit to Gandhi's ashram, which inspired him to set up the Gandhian Community of the Arch in France. Originally published as *Pele rinage aux Sources*, Denoel, 1943.

462. Desai, Narayan. *Towards a Nonviolent Revolution.* Rajghat, Varanasi: Sarva Seva Sangh Prakashan. 1972. 167.

Essays on the role of the Gandhian Shanti Sena (Peace Brigade) in India in 1970 and the new society it is trying to create.

463. Masani, R. P. *The Five Gifts.* London: Collins, 1957. 192.

Covers the Land Gift Movement, led by Vinoba Bhave, up to 1954.

464. Narayan, Jayaprakash. *Socialism, Sarvodaya and Democracy.* Edited by Bimla Prasad. London: Asia Publishing House, 1985. 287.

A selection of Narayan's speeches from 1936 to 1961.

465. Narayan, Jayaprakash. *A Revolutionary Quest: Selected Writings of Jayaprakash Narayan.* Edited by Bimla Prasad. Delhi: Oxford University Press, 1980. 406.

466. Ostergaard, G., and M. Currell. *The Gentle Anarchists.* Oxford: Clarendon Press, 1971. 421.

Assessment of Vinoba Bhave and his Land Gift (Bhoodan Movement), trying to promote social change through nonviolent persuasion and eschewing party politics.

467. Ostergaard, Geoffrey. *Nonviolent Revolution in India.* New Delhi: Gandhi Peace Foundation, 1985. Also published London: Housmans, 1985.

Account of the movement to give land to landless labourers and set up village communities on Gandhian lines led by Vinoba Bhave and Jayaprakash Narayan.

468. Ram, Suresh. *Vinoba: The Economics of the Bhoodan Movement.* Varanasi: Sarva Seva Sangh, 1962. 516.

469. Shepard Mark. *Gandhi Today: The Story of Mahatma Gandhi's Successors.* Washington, D.C.: Seven Locks Press, 1987. 145.

470. Tennyson, Hallam. *Saint on the March: The Story of Vinoba.* London: Gollancz, 1955. 223.

471. Tinker, Hugh. *Reorientation: Studies on Asia in Transition.* London: Pall Mall Press, 1965. 175.

Chapter 9, "Magnificent Failure? The Gandhian Ideal in India," assesses how far Gandhism has been practised in India since Gandhi's death. Published earlier in *International Affairs*, 40, 1964: 262–76.

See also Alan and Wendy Scarfe, *JP: His Biography* (Section III.B)

Articles

472. Naik, J.P . "Development of Gandhian Tradition in India." *Review of Politics* 45 (July 1983): 345–65.

XII. Bibliographies and General Reference Works

XII. A. Gandhi Bibliographies

473. Despande, Pandurang Ganesh. *Gandhiana: A Bibliography of Gandhian Literature*. Ahmedabad: Navajivan, 1948. 239.

474. Indian Council of Social Science Research. *Mohandas Karamchand Gandhi: A Bibliography*. New Delhi: Orient Longman, 1974. 379.

Annotated bibliography of books on Gandhi in English up to 1972, including table of contents of each book. 1,095 items, subject and author indices. Introduced by R. R. Diwakar.

475. Kovalsky, Susan J. *Mahatma Gandhi and his Political Influence in South Africa*. Johannesburg: University of the Witwatersrand, 1971. 27. Mimeo.

476. Satyaprakash. *Gandhiana 1962–1976*. New Delhi: Indian Documentation Service, 1977. 184.

Compilation of 2,652 articles, research papers, notes, news and book reviews from 100 Indian English-language journals and from the daily *Times of India*.

477. Sharma, Jagdish Saran. *Mahatma Gandhi: A Descriptive Bibliography*. Delhi: S. Chand, 1955. 565. Second edition 1968, 650.

The original edition has 3,671 entries of which about 90 percent are English language titles, but books and articles in other European languages are included. The second edition incorporates an additional 918 entries of material published between 1954 and 1968, including many in Indian languages, inserted as Vol. 2. There are also an introductory essay and chronology. General biographies are listed according to year of publication. The bulk of the bibliography is arranged by subject.

478. Vir, Dharma. *Gandhi Bibliography*. Chandigarh: Gandhi Smarak Nidhi, 1967. 575.

Vir lists 3,485 entries including poems and novels about Gandhi, paintings and photographic collections and 253 books read by Gandhi as well as biographies and accounts of Gandhi's thought.

See also: Joan Bondurant, *Conquest of Violence*, pp. 249–56; Gene Sharp, *Gandhi as a Political Strategist*, Appendix D, pp. 328–41. (Section IX.)

XII. B. General Reference Works

479. *Biography Index*. New York: H.W. Wilson Co. 1947–

The first two volumes (1947–1949 and 1949–1952) include substantial references to Gandhi, and succeeding volumes have usually included some reference.

480. *International Index: A Guide to Periodical Literature in the Social Sciences and Humanities*. New York: H.W. Wilson Co. Vols. 1–18. 1907–1965.

Lists articles from a range of both scholarly and general interest periodicals. Not annotated. References to Gandhi begin to appear from l919 and become frequent from 1920. There are a few earlier references to the nonviolent campaigns in South Africa.

481. *Social Sciences and Humanities Index.* New York: H.W. Wilson Co. Vols. 19–27. 1965–1974.

Continuation of the *International Index.*

482. *Social Sciences Index.* New York: H.W. Wilson Co. Nos. 1–. 1975–

Continuation of the *Social Sciences and Humanities Index.* A companion *Humanities Index* has also been published annually by H. W. Wilson from 1975.

XII. C. Brief Biographical Entries in Reference Works

483. *The Blackwell Encyclopaedia of Political Thought.* ed. David Miller. Oxford: Basil Blackwell, 1987.

Brief resume of Gandhi's life and a clear summary of his key ideas, plus a balanced assessment of his achievements and limitations written by Bhiku Parekh (pp. 173–74).

484. *Chambers Biographical Dictionary.* ed. Magnus Magnusson. Edinburgh: Chambers, 1990.

Very brief entry referring to Gandhi's *Autobiography* (p. 565).

485. *The Fontana Dictionary of Modern Thinkers.* eds. Alan Bullock and R. B. Woodings. London: Fontana, 1983. 867.

Very brief critical entry on Gandhi, misleading on Gandhi's attitude to partition (pp. 256–57).

486. *The International Dictionary of Twentieth Century Biography.* eds. Edward Vernoff and Rima Shore. London: Sidgwick and Jackson, 1987.

One paragraph entry on Gandhi recommending books by Fischer, Payne, Erikson and Bondurant (p. 244).

487. *Longman Dictionary of Twentieth Century Biography*. ed. Alan Isaacs and Elizabeth Martin. Harlow: Longman, 1985.

Very brief summary of Gandhi's life (p. 195).

488. *The Macmillan Dictionary of Biography*. eds. Barry Owen Jones and M. V. Dixon. London: Macmillan, 1989. New and revised edition.

A rather more substantial biographical entry than in some other dictionaries including recommended reading (pp. 329–30).

489. *Who Was Who 1941–1950*. Vol. 4. London: Adam and Charles Black, 1952.

One paragraph entry (p. 419).

List of Periodicals Referenced

This is a list of weekly, fortnightly, monthly and quarterly general interest periodicals that have carried articles about Gandhi cited in this bibliography, together with more specialised periodicals and academic journals ranging across a number of disciplines. Some of these periodicals published in the 1920s and 1930s, for example, *Amerasia*, no longer exist. Publishers of journals may also have changed over time. Places of publication given here are linked to the period of the article(s) cited, and are intended partly as a guide to the country in which the journal has been or is being published. Almost all periodicals listed are either British or American, although a few periodicals or academic journals published in other parts of the world are included, among them two Indian history journals. For information on Gandhi's own periodicals, and on South African and Indian newspapers and periodicals that reported on Gandhi's campaigns, see Section I.

Amerasia, New York, N.Y.

American Academy of Religion. Journal, Chico, Calif.

American Film, Washington, D.C.

American Journal of Economics and Sociology, New York, N.Y.

American Review, Bloomington, Ill.

American Scholar, Washington, D.C.

Les Annales Politiques et Litteraires, Paris

Asia, New York, N.Y.

Asiatic Review new series, London

Atlantic Monthly, Boston, Mass.

Blackwoods Magazine, New York, N.Y.

British Journal of Sociology, London

Canadian Journal of Political Science, Waterloo, Ont.

Catholic World, New York, N.Y.

Century, New York, N.Y.

China Weekly Review, Shanghai

Christian Century, Chicago, Ill.

Church Quarterly Review, London

Commentary, New York, N.Y.

Contemporary Review, London

Cornhill Magazine, London

Cross Currents, West Nyack, N.Y.

Current Anthropology, Chicago, Ill.

Current History, Magazine of the New York Times, New York, N.Y.

Current Opinion, New York, N.Y.

Deutsche Rundschau, Berlin

Encounter, London

Ethics, Chicago, Ill.

Far Eastern Economic Review, New York, N.Y.

Fortnightly Review, London

Forum, New York, N.Y.

Great Britain and the East, London

Hibbert Journal, London

History and Theory, Middletown, Conn.

History Today, London

Independent and Weekly Review, New York, N.Y.

The Indian Economic and Social History Review, Delhi

The Indian Historical Review, Delhi

Institute of World Affairs Proceedings, Los Angeles, Calif.

International Philosophical Quarterly, New York, N.Y.

International Review of Missions, London

International Review of Social History, Amsterdam

Jewish Affairs, Johannesburg

Journal des Debats, Paris

Journal of Applied Sociology, Los Angeles

The Journal of Asian Studies, Ann Arbor, Mich.

Journal of Asian and African Studies, Leiden, Netherlands

Journal of Conflict Resolution, Beverley Hills, Calif.

Journal of Economic Issues, Lincoln, Neb.

The Journal of Ethnic Studies, Bellingham, Wash.

Journal of European Studies, London

Journal of International Relations, Baltimore, Md.

Journal of Modern African Studies, Cambridge

Journal of the History of Ideas, New York, N.Y.

Journal of Peace Research, Oslo, Norway

Journal of World History, New York, N.Y. (UNESCO)

Journalism Quarterly, Minneapolis, Minn.

Labour Monthly, London

Living Age, Boston, Mass.

Literary Digest, New York, N.Y.

London Quarterly Review, London

Methodist Review, New York, N.Y.

Missionary Review of the World, New York, N.Y.

Nation, New York, N.Y.

National Review, London

Near East and India, London

New England Quarterly, Brunswick, Maine

New Republic, Washington, D.C.

New Statesman (later New Statesman and Nation), London

Open Court, Chicago, Ill.

Outlook, New York, N.Y.

Pacific Affairs, Vancouver

Pacific Historial Review, Berkeley, Calif.

Partisan Review, New York, N.Y.

Peace and Change, Newley Park, Calif.

Philosophy East and West, Honolulu, Hawaii

Political Quarterly, London

Political Studies, Oxford

Quarterly Review, New York, N.Y.

Religious Studies, New York, N.Y.

Review of Politics, Notre Dame, Ind.

Review of Reviews, New York, N.Y. (1920s references)

Revue de Paris, Paris

Round Table, London

The Russian Review, Hanover, N.H.

Social Forces, Baltimore, Md.

Social Policy, White Plains, N.Y.

Sociology and Social Reserch, Los Angeles, Calif.

South Atlantic Quarterly, Durham, N.C.

Spectator, London

Theology Today, Princeton, N.J.

Thought, New York, N.Y.

Victorian Studies, Bloomington, Ind.

Virginia Quarterly Review, Charlottesville, Va.

Westermanns Monatschefte, Berlin

Western Political Quarterly, Salt Lake City, Utah

World Politics, Princeton, N.J.

World Tomorrow, New York, N.Y.

Glossary of Indian Terms

The terms listed below are often found in Gandhian text and books about Gandhi.

advaita: Hindu philosophical school of thought believing in monism, not the duality of the divine and the earthly

ahimsa: non-injury; nonviolence; defined by Gandhi as "not merely a negative state of harmlessness but . . . a positive state of love" (*Young India*, 19 January 1921)

ashram: spiritual community or retreat often centred on a spiritual teacher; Gandhi's ashrams served a spiritual function but were also centres for experiments in the constructive programme and bases for Gandhi's political campaigns

bania: member of caste of traders (Gandhi belonged to Modh Bania subcaste)

Bapu: father; affectionate style of address often used for Gandhi

Bhoodan:	land-gift; movement led by Vinoba Bhave after Gandhi's death asking landowners to give some of their land to landless peasants
bramacharaya:	celibacy
Brahmin:	member of the highest, priestly caste in Hinduism
charka:	spinning wheel
darshan:	sight of holy person that results in benediction (peasants would try to catch a glimpse of Gandhi or attend huge outdoor meetings to receive his darshan)
dharma:	duty; Hindu moral code; religion
dhoti:	loincloth (worn by Gandhi to signal identification with poor)
duragraha:	stubborn persistence, coercive resistance such as strikes or boycotts (as opposed to Gandhian satyagraha)
guru:	holy man, spiritual teacher
harijan:	Gandhi's coinage for the untouchables (outcasts), meaning literally child of God; name of Gandhi's periodical founded in 1933
hartal:	form of brief strike and shutting down of businesses, an ancient form of popular protest; also a form of national mourning; often used by Gandhi
himsa:	violence or wish to harm (see ahimsa)
karma:	law of ethical causation
khadi:	hand-spun cloth (central element in Gandhi's constructive programme)
lathi:	metal-tipped cane used by the Indian police

Mahatma:	"Great Soul"; Hindu title of respect bestowed on Gandhi by Tagore
mandir:	temple; Gandhi in letters from Yeravda jail in the 1930s referred to it as "Yeravda mandir"
Maulana:	title applied to Muslim learned man; for example, Maulana Azad
navajivan:	new life; name of Gandhi's Gujarati periodical and his publishing house
panchayat:	small local council that has been popularly elected
Pandit:	honorific title applied to Brahmins; for example, Pandit Nehru
raj:	rule; "British raj" used to denote British imperial rule in India; "panchayat raj" means village democracy
sabha:	assembly, association
Sardar:	honorific title meaning nobleman; for example, Sardar Patel
sangh:	fellowship, association
sarvodaya:	the welfare of all; term used by Gandhi for his social philosophy
satya:	truth
satyagraha:	truth-force; Gandhi's distinctive form of nonviolent resistance based on voluntary suffering and adherence to the truth; but also used more loosely to describe nonviolent campaigns associated with Gandhi
satyagrahi:	practitioner of nonviolent resistance
swadeshi:	belonging to or made in one's own country; policy of economic self-reliance, in particular, using only Indian cloth

swaraj: self-rule; independence

taluka: administrative subdivision of district, region composed of villages

varna: caste

Author Index

Indexed by item numbers. Names of editors included (except for general reference works Sections XII.B and XII.C)

Subject Index

This index covers key events and issues in Gandhi's life and central themes in his thought. It also includes individual thinkers and political leaders relevant to understanding his life and thought and lists his close companions. Since Gandhi himself is covered throughout, he has been excluded. Entries are based entirely on specific references in this bibliography. The index refers to item numbers.

About the Author

APRIL CARTER is Senior Lecturer in the Department of Government at the University of Queensland. She has written books on political theory, women's rights, and arms control. She has also compiled *Nonviolent Action: A Selected Bibliography* (1970) and *Marshal Tito: A Bibliography* (1989).

ISBN 0-313-28296-X

90000>

EAN

9 780313 282966

HARDCOVER BAR CODE